WHAT PEOPLE ARE S

ASTRO-CHARACTERS

A fascinating read and wonderful aid for every kind of writer. In a world where so many fictionalised characters have "bolt-on eccentricities" that rarely ring true, Judy's book gives you all the tools you need to give characters layers that are not only interesting but also entirely credible.
Tim John, screenwriter and author.

Judy Hall's *ASTRO-CHARACTERS* fills a crucial niche in an otherwise stacked-to-the-gills library of writers' guides. She writes in an approachable, no-nonsense style which both echoes and enriches her subject matter. Any would-be writer starting work on a new book would be well advised to consult *ASTRO-CHARACTERS* and follow its sage advice. I've been constructing astro-charts for my main characters for years now, and find it an immensely useful tool for keeping tabs on elusive protagonists. I particularly liked the author's Crib Sheets section – her Leo notes are very close to the bone indeed! A thoroughly well-written and well-researched book by an experienced author which should grace any aspiring writer's bookshelf.
Mario Reading, author, *The Anti-Christ Trilogy.*

I absolutely loved this book, found it fascinating from the very beginning. I thought the concept was original and brilliant. I could almost see the characters appearing as the traits were described. Loved the questionnaire character builder and the inclusion of the sex styles – really helpful for romance writers I would think as well as writers in general. I just thought the whole thing was so different. Can't wait to see it in print. I think it would be considered a desk top essential as you write.
Tracy Baines, author and creative writing tutor.

Astro-characters

A writer's guide to creating
compelling fictional characters with
the signs of zodiac

Astro-characters

A writer's guide to creating
compelling fictional characters with
the signs of zodiac

Judy Hall

**COMPASS
BOOKS**

Winchester, UK
Washington, USA

First published by Compass Books, 2013
Compass Books is an imprint of John Hunt Publishing Ltd., Laurel House, Station Approach,
Alresford, Hants, SO24 9JH, UK
office1@jhpbooks.net
www.johnhuntpublishing.com
www.compass-books.net

For distributor details and how to order please visit the 'Ordering' section on our website.

Text copyright: Judy Hall 2013

ISBN: 978 1 78279 243 7

A CIP catalogue record for this book is available from the British Library.

Design: Stuart Davies

Printed and bound by CPI Group (UK) Ltd, Croydon, CR0 4YY

We operate a distinctive and ethical publishing philosophy in all
areas of our business, from our global network of authors to
production and worldwide distribution.

CONTENTS

In loving memory of Angela Sewell (Virgo, 1928-2012), writer and raconteur extraordinaire, who kept me on my toes and taught me that you can have dialogue with only one character present. Keep dancing on that bar in heaven lovely lady!

Introduction

Convincing Characters

'Now for the hitch in Jane's character,' he said at last, speaking more calmly than from his look I had expected him to speak. 'The reel of silk has run smoothly enough so far; but I always knew there would come a knot and a puzzle: here it is. Now for vexation, and exasperation, and endless trouble!'
Jane Eyre Charlotte Brontë (Taurus sun, Aquarius moon)

Does that quotation from *Jane Eyre* draw you in? Intrigue you? Does it make you want to discover more about the 'knot and puzzle' in an otherwise silken woman? It does me. Those three sentences sum up the character of Jane perfectly. This paragon of virtue has hidden depths to be revealed. Even though the language is archaic, I'm hooked. It fills me with glee at the delights to come. I want to know more about *who, what* and *why*. Three vital ingredients of a story.

Vibrant characters are essential to any story. It's people who drive a plot. Their conflicts, strengths, weaknesses, internal struggles, challenges, dilemmas and resiliencies are the raw material of any tale. I'm going to call them characters even though Ernest Hemingway (Cancer sun, Capricorn moon, Virgo rising) insisted that a character is a caricature but this isn't necessarily so. He advised that a writer should create real people instead. As we shall see, you can quickly create a real person who will jump off the page and resonate with your readers. That person will have a memorable – and believable – personality. You just need a bit of astrological know-how and guidance from the zodiac signs themselves. In the astrological profiles that follow the signs share their most intimate secrets and the flaws and foibles that make them so fascinating for writers and their readers. The zodiac archetypes are so characteristic and instantly identifiable they resonate with the reader at an almost subconscious level. Fortunately you don't need to know anything about astrology to use zodiac traits to bring your characters to life.

Mario Reading, best selling author of *The Antichrist Trilogy* always creates birth charts and horoscopes for his characters. 'It gives me a deeper insight into their motivation and character' he explains, 'and I find it an immensely useful tool for keeping tabs on elusive protagonists.' Exactly what I do myself when writing fictional characters – and whenever I read a book, or watch visual drama. Within the first few minutes I've mentally allocated each character to a zodiac sign (the *who*). But, as you'll discover, there is more than just the sun-sign to consider. I find the characters that hold my attention and feel authentic are invariably ones that stay aligned to 'their sign' – but the protagonist will also reveal two other astrological factors, a rising sign (the *what*) and a moon sign (the *why*). This is what adds the 'knots and puzzles' to a character, creating multi-layers, and we'll be delving deeper into this in Chapter 1 and looking further into the astro-characters in *Jane Eyre* in Chapter 2.

Writing perfection?

> The psyche consists essentially of images. It is a series of images in the truest sense, not an accidental juxtaposition or sequence, but a structure that is throughout full of meaning and purpose.
> 'Spirit & Love', (Collected Works VIII) Carl Jung (Leo sun, Taurus moon, Aquarius rising)

It's a cliché but it's true that your readers must engage with your character(s). Their attention has to be grabbed and the fate of your protagonist has to matter to them, otherwise they'll stop reading. This is true of even minor protagonists. But don't make your characters too perfect. As writer and humourist Mark Twain (Sagittarius sun, Aries moon, Scorpio rising) wisely said, "I haven't a particle of confidence in a man who has no redeeming petty vices whatsoever." All the zodiac signs have their quirks and their shadow side. When the nineteenth-century politician Lord Macaulay (Scorpio sun, Taurus moon) tells us that 'the measure of a man's real character is what he would do if he knew he would never be found out' he's referring to what writers – and their readers – find so fascinating: the darker side of human nature. Shadows and foibles, smoke and mirrors, make compelling reading but characters must also have something likeable about them, a redeeming feature that draws in the reader. Even the worst villain must evoke an empathetic response somewhere along the line if your story is to be successful. Astrology shows you both faces, offering clues as to how that archetypal bad boy can dearly love his old mum and obey her every word and yet create mayhem of which she would not be proud, and have women falling at his feet all at the same time. The biggest rogue can suddenly make an unexpected stand on a matter of principle or the stoniest heart perform a random act of kindness.

As a writer you need to know your characters inside out – and yet be willing to be surprised. To allow a little serendipity into their – and your – life. They must fit the plot and be realistic. Your character requires background and backstory (the moon, we'll come to this shortly) – even if this is only hinted at in your actual tale. They need a worldview: the lens through which your character perceives the world (the rising sign of which more in a moment). The zodiac signs in which the sun (the sun-sign) and moon (the moon-sign) were placed at birth provide the *raison d'etre* for your character's visceral reactions and hold the key to internal tensions and conflicts. Protagonists need to struggle and come to some sort of resolution. By putting your characters through challenge and pain, you are not being sadistic. You're giving them – and your readers – a gift. It provides an opportunity to develop nascent qualities. This is the way your characters take on deeper meaning, they evolve and grow. They become compelling and *real*.

Motivation is crucial. Conflicting motivation between two characters creates tension in a story, as does one person facing an external dilemma or internal struggle. When creating a character ask yourself what is this person's fundamental passion, fear and desire? What drives your protagonist? What is the body language that expresses this? How does this person think? This is where astrology comes in!

Astrologers have been observing human nature since the beginning of time, as have writers. All writers observe people, store scraps of dialogue, note traits and quirks and predominant emotions to weave into authentic characters. They bear in mind that a public face can be quite different to the private person, amalgamating several facets into a character to multi-layer it. Using astrology takes this a step further and makes the process more intentional. Because astrology draws on ancient behavioural patterns deeply ingrained in the human psyche, your protagonist will be totally believable. The astro-profiles give you a pithy foundation on which to build. Each astro-profile opens with a quotation that sums up the sign but which may not be by a writer from that sign (the author's astrological information is included where known).

So, the good news is that astrology, through the twelve basic sun signs, can help you to achieve greater authenticity in your characters and the great news is that, by taking your use of astrology just two simple steps further – adding a moon and rising sign – you can refine the twelve broad principles into a unique understanding of the inner workings of your character's personality, quirks, thoughts, feelings, motivation and behaviour. The resulting synergy goes way beyond the separate components to create something uniquely individual with all the inherent foibles, angst, aptitudes and internal tensions that you need in a compelling character. Perfect!

Enjoy your writing,
Judy Hall

Chapter I

How to Use this Book

Forming characters! Whose? Our own or others? Both. And in that momentous fact lies the peril and responsibility of our existence.

Elihu Burritt (Sagittarius sun, Taurus moon)

The signs of the zodiac can be looked on as archetypes: recurrent motifs deeply ingrained in the human psyche that drive human behaviour. These archetypes have been described for at least three thousand years so it's no wonder readers identify with them. The zodiac archetypes broadly delineate how someone born under each sun-sign will act, think and feel and they don't shy away from the darker, hidden sign of human nature. In ancient times the signs were given names that not only resembled the zodiac constellations in the sky but also described the temperament that went with each zodiac personality. The profiles in this book are drawn with a somewhat jaundiced eye, delineating the darker facets of the signs but that's what makes them useful to writers – and interesting to readers. We don't want to stay on the surface. We need to incorporate quirks, flaws and foibles to make our protagonists authentic – and intriguing.

Celestial archetypes

Aries is the Ram and those horns head-butt their way through life.

Taurus is the Bull: strong and slow to anger but watch out when it charges.

Gemini is the Twins: the first human sigil in the zodiac and oh how the twins love to share ideas.

Cancer is the Crab with the tough shell, soft underbelly, and claws that hold on tight.

Leo is the Lion: proud leader of the pack.

Virgo is now the Virgin, pure and chaste, but this used to be the fruitful Corn Maiden so there's an erotic undertone and huge internal struggle.

Libra is the only inanimate sigil, those Scales judge and weigh things in the balance, swinging wildly until equilibrium is found.

Scorpio is the mesmerising Scorpion, watch out for the vicious sting in the tail.

Sagittarius is the Centaur-Archer that combines animal and human, instinct and intellect, and lets fly that arrow wherever it will.

Capricorn is the Goat. Fleet footed mountain goats quickly make it to the top whilst their domesticated cousins stay corralled within tight limits. In the old Babylonian zodiac, Capricorn was the sea goat with a tail in the waters of the unconscious and head in the intellectual air realm above, blending intuition with reason.

Aquarius, the Water Bearer, pours out the waters of life but tends to be a detached observer of the life that feelings create.

Imaginative, escapist **Pisces** is summed up by its two interlinked Fishes swimming in opposite directions but forever tied together.

The astro-profiles in this book are built on how the signs will behave, think, speak and feel under different circumstances. This behaviour is embedded deep in the human psyche. Two millennia ago, Marcus Manilius, a Stoic philosopher, described the zodiac characters:

The Ram [Aries] will ever cherish hopes, he will rise from the sudden shipwreck of his affairs to abundant wealth only to meet with a fall, and his desires will lead him to disaster, he will yield his produce for the common good. The Ram has a diffident heart that ever yearns to commend itself by its own praise.

The Bull [Taurus] demands a yoke for its shoulders and neither pauses in the furrows nor relaxes its breast in the dust. Their hearts and bodies derive strength from a massiveness that is slow to move, whilst in their faces dwells the boy-god Love.

The Twins [Gemini] find even work a pleasure, theirs is a life of ease and unfading youth spent in the arms of love. They also discover new paths to the skies. Nature yields to their genius. So many are the accomplishments of which the Twins is fruitful.

The Crab [Cancer] has a grasping spirit and, unwilling to give itself in service, the Crab distributes many kinds of gain, and skill in making profits. He sells seasons of idleness at rates of interest to his liking. His is a shrewd nature and he is ready to fight for his profits.

The Lion [Leo] filled with the urge to adorn their proud portals with pelts spending their lives on spoil and pillaging of stocks. They swagger about to meet the demands of luxury. Their temper is prone to fitful wrath and ready withdrawal and guileless are the sentiments of their honest hearts.

The Virgin [Virgo] minds trained in the learned arts. The impulse to investigate the causes and effects of things. On them she will confer a tongue which charms, the mastery of words, and that mental vision which can discern all things however concealed they may be. Bashfulness handicaps the early years of such persons.

The Scales [Libra] acquainted with the tablets of law, he will know what is permissible and the penalties incurred by doing what is forbidden. Whatever stands in dispute and needs a ruling the pointer of the balance will determine.

The Scorpion [Scorpio] creates natures ardent for war and active service, and a spirit which rejoices in plenteous bloodshed and in carnage more than in plunder.

The Centaur [Sagittarius] delights in imposing a master on every kind of quadruped and taming them. It imparts keenness to the intellect, swiftness of movement and an indefatigable spirit.

Capricorn smelts out riches and folds surehanded the malleable mass. Has a fondness for clothes and wares which dispel the cold. The first half of the sign has a fondness for love and is charged with guilt, the second half has a virtuous old age.

The youthful Waterman [Aquarius] bestows skills such as how to divine springs from under the ground. They who issue from this sign are a gentle and lovable breed and no meanness of heart is theirs; they are prone to suffer losses; and of riches they have neither need nor surfit [sic]. Even thus doth the urn's stream flow.

The Fishes [Pisces] possess a love of the sea. They hide the hook within the bait or the guile within the weel [sic]. The children of this sign have a friendly disposition, swiftness of movement and live where everything is ever apt to change.

(Extracted from Manilius, *Astronomica*)

Descriptions which today would be recognised by astrologers and which are of inestimable value to writers as a reader will instinctively recognise a zodiac-based character.

Astro-personalities

And there appeared a great wonder in heaven, a woman clothed with the sun, and the moon under her, and upon her head a crown of twelve stars.
Revelations 12:1

For most people astrology is what they read in their 'stars', daily or monthly horoscopes. Such predictions may hint at an astro-personality and each sign's idiosyncratic quirks with comments such as 'your love of gossip' (Gemini) 'your secretive sign ... ' (Scorpio), 'your brutal honesty ... ' (Sagittarius) or 'your romantic nature ... ' (Pisces), but give no indication of what astrology really offers an author. This ancient technique has consistently mapped the vagaries of the human psyche. It gives you a unique insight into people and makes your protagonists leap off the page. No matter how surprising, their behaviour will always be in character.

Writers are very familiar with the process of creating – and dissecting – complexity. We have to be intimate with all the hidden corners of our characters' to fully reveal all their layers. We need to know our characters darkest secrets, their backstory, their hopes and dreams, their struggles and challenges. I believe we can only be truly intimate – and our protagonists authentic – if we are completely honest with the reader, holding nothing of the character back out of fear or favour – although you can of course sneakily hold back for the purpose of creating intrigue and impact at the appropriate moment.

Intimacy is about opening and sharing yourself on all levels with someone *other*. In the case of writers it is about sharing our characters with our readers, but it also involves sharing ourselves with our characters. All writers advertently or inadvertently put something of themselves into their creations. So intimacy is how close you as a writer can allow someone to come to your character, and how deeply you can share your character's thoughts and feelings, passions and aversions, prejudices and foibles. To be intimate, you have to surrender yourself. Which makes writers vulnerable, so trust is essential for such intimacy. Trust in the process of creativity, trust in our readers, trust in our characters. For some sun-signs this is easy, but for other, more suspicious or introverted signs, intimacy and trust are an enormous challenge. So, writing certain characters will be more challenging than others. Both from your own point of view, according to your personal astrology, and that of your protagonist. But, whichever sign you choose for your character, astrology throws light into the most complex of personalities.

The zodiac profiles

You stars that reigned at my nativity
Whose influence hath allotted death and hell
Dr Faustus Christopher Marlowe

Each zodiac profile gives you an outline of essential traits for a particular sun sign. A 'crib-sheet' comes first. A thumb nail sketch that gives you an instant identity kit: first impression, appearance, dress, stance, verbal style, likes and dislikes and so on. Incorporate these and already you will have an identifiable character that resonates with your reader. But to add depth, and to place your character in role in the story, this is followed by the zodiac sign itself giving you a more in-depth look at its personality style, what makes that sign tick and what a male or female character with that sun-sign would reveal to you. For each sign there is an example of 'astro-speak' taken from blogs, emails or real-life conversations in which someone with the sun in that sign speaks their truth.

While each sun-sign shares specific characteristics, certain traits will reveal themselves more in one type of relationship than another – lover, co-worker or friend – each of which can be incorporated into your writing. So 'getting to know me' is followed by the sign letting you in on how it acts in love and partnership, friendship and as a co-worker together with a compatibility rating with other signs so that you can introduce tension or harmony between your characters as required. It's up to you to decide how honest that zodiac sign is being with you – some withhold themselves much more than others, letting you only catch sideways glimpses of their true nature. But the language they use will tell you a great deal about how they view themselves and how willing they are to let you enter into their world. Read the spaces between the words to gain the deepest insight.

The sun is only part of your character's own unique self. The qualities that character brings to a relationship or environment are modified by other factors as we will see (which take into account time and place of birth but don't worry, you can use artistic licence) so in the Astro-profiles the moon in a zodiac sign and as the rising-sign mask reveal their secrets to you. However, from the sun-sign alone, it is possible to build a believable, although somewhat shallow, character base and to predict how that character will behave.

What a sun-sign tells you

A man's character may be learned from the adjectives which he habitually uses in conversation.
Mark Twain (Sagittarius sun, Aries moon, Scorpio rising)

The zodiac sign under which someone was born represents a particular approach to life which is broadly shared with everyone born under that sign – although in some cases it can be hidden by the rising sign mask. In astrology, this is called the sun-sign. How your characters' drives are expressed and how much they share themselves with others is shown by the sun-sign. Some signs are introverted, shy and retiring, others are extravert, full on and unstoppable. Certain sun-signs initiate, or respond, others react; some live in the inner world of the imagination, others in the external world of action. There are signs that are uninhibited exhibitionists whilst others take a great deal of coaxing to reveal their desires.

Choose a birthday for your characters and as a writer you instantly know their personality, their secret hopes and dreams, their strengths and weaknesses, their internal struggles, their vocabulary, how they look, the mask they put on to meet the world, and how they act in friendship or adversity and in love. Each sign has a particular body language and distinctive appearance. To see a typical Aries take a look, for instance, at William Bell Scott's painting of the poetic writer Algernon Swinburne with his wayward curly auburn hair and slanting eyebrows above hypnotic eyes, or the caricature of him by 'Ape' in *Vanity Fair* (both images are on Wikipedia). He had the sun and moon in heroic Aries and romantic, escapist Pisces rising explains the mesmeric eyes.

When facing opposition, plucky Aries squares up ready to do battle, fists metaphorically – or literally – raised; whilst the much-slower-to-anger Taurus head goes down, like a bull about to charge. When the Taurus foot starts pawing the ground, sensible signs withdraw – fast. Light on the feet, Gemini dances around and lets fly a string of words, but Cancer folds both arms over the solar plexus and scuttles sideways avoiding head-on confrontation while Libra takes on an appeasing stance. Leo quells rebellion with a regal look, Scorpio with a penetrating stare. That Aries person will have emphatic eyebrows that meet in the middle, the Taurus a large head set on a strong neck above wide shoulders and tapering legs, the bright-eyed Gemini is darting, bird-like; while the Cancer face resembles the moon and Libra looks good at any time. But how your character looks is not only a product of the sun-sign, it can be masked by another factor, the rising-sign, which we'll come to in a moment.

Adding complexity

> People do not seem to realize that their opinion of the world is also a confession of character.
> Ralph Waldo Emerson (Gemini sun, Leo moon, Libra rising)

The beauty of astro-characterisation is that you add in variables to give an appearance and approach to the world that can mask the innate sun-sign traits, creating conflicts and complexities, leaving more to discover and intrigue. Each zodiac entry has a compatibility chart at the end. This not only tells you which signs interact well or clash with the sign you have chosen for your character but it also gives you subtle complexities and permutations through the inclusion in your protagonist of traits from two more zodiac signs creating internal tensions and dilemmas.

This complex layering can answer one of the most perplexing relationship questions there is: why did two characters get together in the first place? Two people who outwardly seem to have nothing in common are drawn to each other like magnets. They will say that, deep down, they recognised each other. Very often this is because the sun and moon signs intertwine and are compatible, or they share the same moon sign. A guy will have, say, the sun in Aries and a woman the moon. At a very deep level they are incredibly similar and share _some_ basic characteristics. They literally each see the other reflected back as though in a mirror and feel 'I've come home'. But this is only on one level. There are also another sun and moon – or sun and sun – placement and two rising signs to take into account. Add in clashing sign traits and you soon begin to realise why 'home' doesn't always feel as comfortable as it might. The facets of the zodiac create attractions, conflicts and tensions within the pair.

Moon sign

The Moon symbolizes our emotional side, dependency and security, our need for home and roots, and our ties to our mothers.

Being a lunar type in a solar world Donna Cunningham (Cancer sun, Aries moon, Libra rising)

As with all characterisation, there is a complex layering in the zodiac. The twelve sun signs give you twelve broad personality types spread throughout the year, but to use only these limited characteristics would result in flat characters with little subtlety or depth. To construct a believable character you also need to factor in one of twelve possible moon signs, the deep place where your character's feelings and emotions reside, where visceral reactions occur, and which are an indication of what nurtures and subconsciously drives your protagonist. The moon is the site of 'old tapes', scripts that hold deeply ingrained patterns of behaviour. As the moon passes through each of the twelve signs during a month this creates one hundred and forty four potential personalities.

Rising sign (the mask)

We may say, without fear of contradiction, that the only sure and dependable guide to the Ascendant [rising sign] where the time of birth is unknown, is an intimate knowledge of character and career … The Ascendant always influences the character in some measure, and its influence can be traced by any student of human nature with an understanding of astrology.

The Brontes and their stars Maud Margesson

You can then select one of twelve possible rising signs to map the way the character will go out to meet the world. All twelve zodiac signs rise over the horizon during a single day, which offers you infinite complexity. The rising sign is what people tend to notice first about someone. It's the mask your character puts on to face the world and it can obscure or emphasise sun-sign traits, bringing forward contradictions and creating powerful dilemmas and challenges. Technically it is to do with the time of birth but you don't need to know the technicalities to make use of it in your writing. You can simply choose for the rising sign the zodiac sign that makes your character most intriguing.

It is this astrological synergy that creates a believable, multi-dimensional character and which can surprise your reader – and you – at the turn of every page and yet remain authentic.

Creating your astro-character

A man's character is his fate.
Heraclitus (540 BC - 480 BC)

Astro-characterisation is surprisingly simple. Read the profiles of the zodiac signs and pick the one that sketches out the main traits you envisage for a protagonist. This will be your character's sun-sign – so choose a birthday within the sun-sign dates. Even if the birthday never appears in your book, you need to know it as it is part of your character's backstory. Backstory is what happened to them before you introduce them to your reader. It's all the traumas, dramas and joys that have brought your character to the present moment and it's what motivates and delineates them. If you want someone who is romantic at heart, for instance, go for Libra or Pisces. Gullible Pisces if you want a back history of broken hearts and relationship muddles, tougher Libra for one of striving for peaceful co-existence or conflict resolution. If you need someone secretive and inscrutable, something of a loner, go for perspicacious Scorpio or possibly authoritarian Capricorn, or, to add a dash of eccentricity to the mix, Aquarius. If your character is a salesperson at heart, silver-tongued Gemini can sell ice to Inuits, and will convince your reader black is white in the process. Putting the signs out of their comfort zones creates interesting reading. Meticulous, fastidious Virgo will not react well to a messy muddle, and a Capricorn who is powerless in an out of control situation goes through serious angst.

Meeting the shadow

It may be asked of course as to why that particular kind of life happened in the first place. And the answer in all cases, for any of us, is rooted, again, in our desire nature. Desires are acted upon. And those desires create reactions to themselves. *Understanding Karmic Complexes* Patricia L. Walsh

Bear in mind that the sun-sign profiles in this book are exaggerated for dramatic effect and that some sad, repressed souls are the very inverse of their sun sign and need to grow into what should be their natural characteristics. Others live out their shadow sides rather more fully than the people around them might like or remain mired in a toxic moon sign – which makes them engrossing for a writer. This struggle to embrace the shadow can be part of their evolution as a protagonist. Some signs have very dark shadow-sides to them. A repressed powerless Leo, for instance, hides in corners or struts his stuff, hates to be seen or perceived as a failure, feels totally inadequate and does anything but shine, manipulating or bullying his or her way through what feels like a thwarted, frustrated life. Or he'll be totally egocentric and demanding, completely disconnected from other people. Left to his own devices he's likely to turn into a dictator running his own mini-country. But this character discovering personal power and presence, learning how to shine and to be a uniquely special individual could drive your story forward.

All the astro-profiles include a sign's shadow qualities, but if you want to add complexity to a sun-sign, think in terms of incorporating the shadow qualities of the sign opposite to it on the zodiac wheel (see below). Signs operate in pairs, so the Aries opposite is Libra, the Taurus opposite is Scorpio, Gemini opposes Sagittarius, Cancer-Capricorn, Leo-Aquarius and Virgo-Pisces. This 'opposition shadow' is often overlooked but it can explain some of the knots and puzzles in a character. Put some Scorpio nastiness into Taurus, for instance, and you've really got something to get your teeth into as a writer. That solid dependability suddenly becomes much more self-centred and power hungry – and incredibly devious. Remembering that Aries is the opposite of Libra makes sense of the fact that, after Libra has adapted and compromised to fit in with everyone else, there is an abrupt breakthrough of selfishness and 'what about my needs' that leaves everyone else reeling; while Libra can suffer from terrible bouts of procrastination and people pleasing. Gentle caring Cancer has the steely determination of Capricorn in its shadow, and Capricorn the emotional vulnerability of Cancer. Virgo can play the put-upon Pisces martyr very well, and Pisces can resort to false humility and fall into fawning servility. Gemini and Sagittarius share an ability to be very economical with the truth.

That's just the start though. To be interesting, characters need to be multi-layered and to hide secrets from the reader, slowly revealing themselves. So now think about your character's emotions and his or her instinctual life, the subconscious forces and needs that drive behaviour – and what your character really doesn't want you to know, the deepest secrets of the psyche that drive them forward regardless of what the conscious mind decides. This is your character's moon-sign. The moon represents ingrained patterns, the 'old tapes' that unconsciously run your character's automatic reactions. The feelings and beliefs they don't always know they have. For interesting characters with plenty of internal angst and tension, you need a moon sign that conflicts with or challenges the sun-sign creating an internal predicament that can be projected onto the outside world. An easy way to do this is to use the compatibility chart at the end of each profile. Or, choose the sign before the sun-sign (bearing in mind that the zodiac wheel is read counter-clockwise), or count on three more counter-clockwise signs, or go to the opposite sign. Don't worry, the astro-wheel shows you exactly what's placed where, see figure 1.

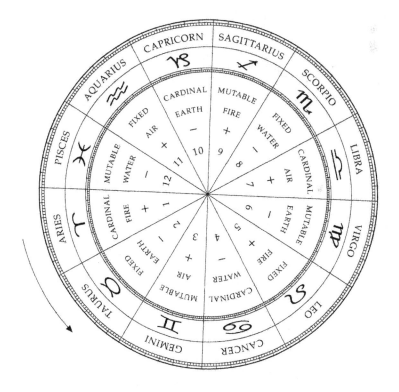

Figure 1: Astro-wheel: read anti-clockwise

So, a straight-forward 'what you see is what you get', me-orientated Aries sun-sign could, for instance, have a highly-emotional, escapist Pisces moon (one sign behind) or a mean and moody, possessive, home-loving Cancer moon (three signs on). Both these moon signs are complex and irrational in the sense of being driven by powerful but unrecognised needs and feelings, which contrasts nicely with the pushy, up front Aries sun and would give your character some interesting complications. If you wanted your protagonist to have a romantic streak, both these moons would heighten the innate Aries romanticism but Cancer hangs on at all costs while Pisces flows fluidly onto the next partner or event – and sometimes forgets to leave the preceding one first. Most Pisces moons lead very complicated lives, although they don't always notice that. If you chose the opposite sign, Libra, you'd have a powerful conflict between the 'I' ego-needs of the sun-sign character and an innate desire to please another person. Libra, with an inclusive urge towards 'us', always takes someone else's views into account and slides from one view to another as the sign tries to keep the peace. Until it collides with overwhelming personal needs. But, Aries' shadow is procrastination so … where does your character go from there?

The third factor to choose is the rising sign – which depends on the time of day someone was born but you don't need to specify this when making your choice, just select a sign with contrasting or strengthening characteristics to the sun and moon sign you have chosen. Remember, the rising sign is the mask your character puts on when going out to meet the world and is an indicator of how other people will view your character. It literally hides the truth of your protagonist until you wish to reveal it. If you want to create more tension in your character's interaction with the environment, or with other characters, a rising sign which contrasts with the sun and moon signs is key. A rising sign that is opposite to or at odds with (i.e. three signs away from) the sun sign characteristics creates misunderstandings and illusions. Tidy, efficient Virgo rising, for instance, covers up the most messy and disorganised of zodiac-signs and your character will never quite understand why other people expect her, or him, to be practical and efficient. A talkative Gemini or confident Leo rising sign can disguise a reticent nature and even though Gemini rising spews out words all the time, these never reveal the true self, nor does the inordinate pride of Leo allow anyone too close too soon.

Exploring the contradictions and duplicities that result from this interplay of sun, moon and rising sign keeps your characters taut. A character, whilst surprising and interesting, will never act unbelievably if you stay within the parameters of these three factors.

Chapter 2

Will an example help? Writing from life

You cannot dream yourself into a character; you must hammer and forge yourself one.

James A. Froude (Taurus sun, Sagittarius moon)

Perhaps an example from real life will help. Take me for instance. I'm a sociable Sagittarius ever ready for adventure, but writing and delving into people's psyche through karmic astrology is an introspective, solitary occupation that fits my Scorpio moon (one sign behind my sun-sign). I have strong intellectual curiosity and started a Masters Degree at the age most people retire, that's my Sagginess. I keep a bag packed – and a guidebook handy – and use Flybe like a bus, also Sag. My novel *Torn Clouds* was based on fifteen trips to Egypt and a lifetime of 'time-slips' into other lives. I read vociferously, the philosophy and esoteric subjects on which I thrive (Sag), but with murder mysteries and historical fiction thrown in for relaxation (Scorpio).

I use examples from my own life all the time in my work (Leo rising), but I doubt that anyone really knows the whole me, they see only the facets that I choose to present – or which they see reflected back to them. You have to know me very well indeed to be let into my secrets. This latter I put down to the secretive Scorpio moon which also accounts for my intense emotions and tendency to brood but you wouldn't know that from my – outwardly – sunny disposition (Leo rising) unless you upset me greatly and then you'll feel the sting in my tail (Scorpio). But as a tell-it-like-it-is, tactless Sag I'm equally likely to upset you with a thoughtless remark or a perceptive but intrusive insight that you'd rather not hear and I simply can't stand lies, deceit and denial which creates an internal struggle because of all that

Scorpio smoke and mirrors. My Scorpio can, however, ferret out your deepest secret and your past – an ability put to good use with the past life astrological readings I offer. My books delve into karma and past lives and explore metaphysics, healing and the unknown.

Like most people with strong Scorpio, although my Sag nature doesn't like to admit it, I hold on to grievances no matter how much I'd like to forgive – so one day I'll be writing *Conversations with the mistress,* a multi-level novel about the traumatic break-up of a pair of contrasting soulmate relationships in the same family. It's been an empty folder on my computer for some time now and writing it will be cathartic (Scorpio). There'll undoubtedly be a barb or three in the tale. But, being a Sag, I'll also use it to highlight the plight of women who as 'common law wives' find that, even after years of loyally supporting a deeply troubled man, they have no rights in law when that partner absconds. I'll explore what happens as they disintegrate before re-finding themselves. With Sag there's always several potential storylines. Mind you, there'll be more than a touch of humour to the story too. My Sag sun and Leo rising have to laugh at life to survive.

With creative, shining, proud Leo as my rising sign I do my fair share of regally surveying a room. It helps me to put on a confident face when I lecture – covering up Scorpionic insecurities – and it's why I feel comfortable appearing on television. The stage is the natural setting for Leo and you have to have more than a touch of actor in you to run workshops and lecture to so many different audiences. My wardrobe reflects my zodiac nature too. Flamboyant Leo stuff for when I'm lecturing or power-dressing to meet a new publisher, appropriate occult attire for Scorpionic rituals, smart-casual Saggy stuff for when I'm out and about, and comfortable trousers and T-shirts for when I'm writing or simply being me. I even have a set of zodiac-festooned tops for when I'm teaching astrology. I well remember being out on a shopping trip with my granddaughter in the pouring rain. We went into a crystal shop and she proudly introduced me as the author of *The Crystal Bible*. 'I didn't think you'd look like that!' said the deeply disappointed shop owner pointing at my dripping cagoule and bedraggled hair. Well ... so what? That Leo-rising might need the right outfit for every occasion, and can use body language to excellent effect, but a Sag sun-sign has to be comfortable and to be *me*. I had no idea I'd be on show and, anyway, I wouldn't have changed how I looked if I had known. Sag needs to be free. My agent and I laugh about a need for big, blonde, bouffant hair in the MBS world, which would suit my Leo rising. But that's one battle my rising sign will never win. It would be a step too far for an insouciant Sag!

Reader, he married her

To the astrologer a door is open that is closed to other enquirers. He can take a glimpse behind the scenes and note the active power at work. He sees not only effects but causes ... How were their [the Bronte's] successes, their failures and their premature deaths foreshadowed in the heavens?
The Brontes and their Stars Maud Margesson

We can take a look too at an example from fiction. The eponymous Jane Eyre with whom I started this book. We don't have a birthday for Jane herself, but we do have the date on which the novel was published. The moment the character was birthed into an unsuspecting world, so I took that as my starting point when analysing her character. The astrology is incredibly synchronistic with what we learn of Jane throughout the book. The publication birthchart has the sun in Libra, the moon in Capricorn and the rising sign is Scorpio if we assume a 9am launch. What a combination! Appropriate astrology for a complex Victorian female character who undergoes great trauma and loss and yet triumphs in the end. The famous (or infamous?) words 'Reader, he married me' that open the last chapter of the novel suggest a romantic Libran conclusion. But before we get to the finale, Jane's Capricorn moon's steely determination to do what she feels is morally right is revealed the further into the novel we plunge. As Jane says: "I can live alone, if self-respect, and circumstances require me so to do. I need not sell my soul to buy bliss. I have an inward treasure born with me, which can keep me alive if all extraneous delights should be withheld, or offered only at a price I cannot afford to give." Expunging her conscience, Jane ventures deep into the Scorpionic underworld before she finds the perfect relationship of which her Libra sun dreams.

As authors we often insert, sometimes unknowingly, a great deal of ourselves into our characters and reflect our own internal tensions. Charlotte Bronte, the author, has been described as 'bossy and controlling' the most dominant and authoritative of the three Bronte sisters. Not surprising with her sun in inflexible, strong minded Taurus and the moon in rebellious and equally strong minded Aquarius, a synergy that, in this case, results in Charlotte's rebellious questioning of convention and strong social criticism that nevertheless has a touch of prejudice. However, she must have been challenged at times by her Leo sister Emily, also an acclaimed 'wildly passionate' author, who – how Leo is this – died aged 29 sitting by the fire combing her long dark hair. However, Emily had her Moon in secretive, vulnerable, protective Cancer and an astrological biographer said of her:

> Emily allowed no stranger's eye to look within and discern her tender spot. When her master set her as an exercise the writing of an imaginary letter to her parents, she allowed her feelings no play. He criticized the production very severely as devoid of all affection and sentiment, and therefore of no

value. Poor Emily – he was asking the impossible of her; it is doubtful whether she could ever have written a really affectionate letter to her father, and she certainly could not have done so under orders from a stranger.

The Brontes and their stars Maud Margesson

Her brother Branwell had his sun tucked beneath a Cancer shell but, more significantly for him, his moon in the self-destructive sign of Scorpio. Towards the end of a short life scarred by drink, drugs and mental illness Branwell wrote:

Backward I look upon my life,
And see one waste of storm and strife,
One wrack of sorrows, hopes, and pain,
Vanishing to arise again!
That life has moved through evening, where
Continual shadows veiled my sphere;
From youth's horizon upward rolled
To life's meridian, dark and cold.

The Bronte family had more than it's share of sorrow and death to deal with. Charlotte herself fell in love with a married man and had to walk away despite her pain, exactly as Jane Eyre does. Jane's harsh experiences at school are based on Charlotte's own. Although married at the time, Charlotte was once described as 'a little, plain, provincial, sickly-looking old maid' and yet pictures of her show strikingly large, dark Taurean eyes. She appears to have associated moral fortitude with plainness, immorality with vanity and good looks.

In Charlotte's novels the outer appearance is always the inverse of the actual nature of the character, so the rising-sign effectively covers up the sun-sign until she's ready to reveal the truth. It's almost as though she understood the workings of astrology. She wasn't afraid to take a risk with her characters and their moral struggles but there can be an air of preachiness about the text – indeed it's been described as a didactical book (a trait of Charlotte's Taurus sun and her character Jane's Capricorn moon). And yet, she makes more than one dig at conventional religion in the book, displaying an intense Aquarian dislike of obsequious hypocrites. In replying to the critics of *Jane Eyre*, Charlotte pointed out in the preface to the second edition:

> Conventionality is not morality. Self-righteousness is not religion. To attack the first is not to assail the last. To pluck the mask from the face of the Pharisee is not to lift an impious hand to the Crown of Thorns ... appearance should not be mistaken for truth.

A perfect summation of a rising-sign.

Charlotte's Aquarian tendency to be way ahead of her time comes out strongly in the novel with her support for the plight of unmarried women and her quiet raging against the restrictions of class and heredity, but so too does her conservative Taurus moon's need to stick to the mores of the time. Charlotte creates a protagonist who values her own moral certainty more than love. Jane Eyre has been described as 'a poor orphan who resisted temptation and saved her honour.' Her story was summed up by one commentator as a harsh childhood controlled by unfeeling adults and having to learn to rely on her own courage and convictions. Let's look at that from an astrological perspective. Jane's moon in Capricorn is the harsh childhood, the poor orphan who is brought up by relatives who feel infinitely superior to Jane, and the cruel, hypocritical and unfeeling school to which she was banished and in which she later taught. That she survived and found her strength is signified by her Scorpio rising sign and that she falls head over heals in love with a conflicted, fascinating man is Libra-Scorpio through and through.

When the man turns out at the altar to have betrayed her by not telling her about his 'mad wife in the attic', instead of storming out Jane discusses the future rationally with him, calming him down and appeasing him: 'the crisis was perilous; but not without its charm: such as the Indian, perhaps, feels when he slips over the rapid in his canoe. I took hold of his [Mr Rochester's] clenched hand, loosened the contorted fingers, and said to him, soothingly — "Sit down; I'll talk to you as long as you like, and hear all you have to say, whether reasonable or unreasonable." The news that he was married was, typically for Scorpio, delivered by a mysterious stranger but there's something seductive about the dangerous drama of the situation that appeals to Jane. It has charm, she takes sly pleasure in it. Jane has diplomatic, peace-loving Libra for her sun-sign. She's a past master at appeasement. But she also has Scorpio for a rising-sign. Scorpio revels in danger and ventures where others fear to tread.

Jane's internal struggle is between a deep need for a passionate relationship at all costs (Libra) combined with the ability to go into all the taboo areas of life (Scorpio) and her conventional Capricorn moon wagging a finger and thundering 'that will never do.' It is that Capricorn moon that won't allow her to give in to Rochester's pleas to run away to the South of France with him even though Libra with another moon-sign would have found a way to wriggle around the moral barrier in the name of love. Her Libra sun somehow overcomes the Scorpionic tendency to hold onto a grudge in that she forgives her betrayer – and, Libra style, berates him for not having more compassion for his mad wife. However, once she makes up her mind that she cannot live with him and put them both outside the mores of society (divorce was not an option when one partner was deemed insane) she is obstinate, obdurate and won't be moved. 'I do love you,' Jane says, 'more than ever: but I must not show or indulge the feeling: and this is the last time I must express it.' A typical Capricorn moon response. Mr Rochester then finds out just how tough Jane is and this is where the quotation with which I opened this book comes in. Up until then he's only seen the submissive, people-pleasing, silken thread Libra side of her nature. Now the knots and puzzles begin to show, the exasperation begins, and she leaves him, plunging into a Scorpionic underworld in which she almost dies before she is rescued by further celestial archetypes.

Morose, tormented and challenging – and once voted the most romantic character in literature – Mr Rochester himself is Scorpio through and through but with more than a touch of Capricorn about him. He could certainly be labelled 'mad, bad and dangerous to know.' This turbulent Byronic character has been described as 'stern featured, craggy-faced, rude, abrupt, horny, twice Jane's age, always on the edge of violence'. His Gothic estate is mysterious, remote and cold and, like the novel itself, has more than a touch of the supernatural about it (Scorpio is very drawn to the occult). He desperately needs to be in control and keeps his poor mad wife locked in the attic rather than place her in an asylum. That she keeps breaking out of her prison and ultimately takes her revenge is his Scorpionness projected out onto his exterior world. Until he meets Jane his feelings are strictly under lock and key but he is more than ready to commit bigamy to gain what he wants which is so Scorpio.

When they meet he tells Jane:

> nature meant me, on the whole, to be a good man, Miss Eyre, one of the better end, and you see I am not so … I am not a villain, you are not to suppose that – not to attribute to me any such bad eminence, but, owing, I verily like to believe, rather to circumstances than to my natural bent, I am a trite common-place sinner, hackneyed in all the poor petty dissipations with which the rich and worthless try to put on life.

A martyred Pisces moon perhaps? Or is it a Capricorn moon

hiding behind Pisces rising?

With her rose-coloured Libran glasses on, Jane describes him as having 'so much unconscious pride in his port, so much case in his demeanour, such a look of complete indifference to his own external appearance, so haughty a reliance on the power of other qualities, intrinsic or adventitious to atone for the lack of mere personal attractiveness, that in looking at him, one inevitably shared the indifference, and even in a blind, imperfect sense, put faith in the confidence.' Maybe we should assign to him a Capricorn rising-sign and a Pisces moon?

But to return to Jane. She describes herself as a plain, Quakerish governess. Very Capricorn moon. And yet she manages to charm the enigmatic, almost misogynistic Rochester into falling passionately in love with her. That rather confirms the Libra with seductive Scorpio rising. Libra can charm the birds out of the trees and yet she does it innocently, naively, in a way which suggests that it was unconscious.

Dialogue reveals a great deal about a character. We've seen how the Libran part of Jane's character uses words to placate – and to convince herself that all is well – but she also has Scorpio's barbed tongue behind her pleasant façade. When the young Jane is taunted with the degradation of her situation by her spoilt brat of a cousin who despises her, she flies into a fury and retorts 'Wicked and cruel boy. You are like a murderer – you are like a slave-driver – you are like the Roman emperors.' She has been reading Goldsmith's *History of Rome* and to her in that moment there is no greater insult and no greater tyrant. She fights the cousin so fiercely that she has to be dragged off and is imprisoned in Scorpionic splendour in the red room in which her uncle died – and which he still haunts. Her behaviour is deemed out of character by one of the maids:

'She never did so before' … said Bessie turning to Abigail.'
But not by the other:

'But it was always in her,' was the reply... 'She's an underhand little thing. I never saw a girl of her age with so much cover.'

Scorpio rising indeed!

Investigating the astrological evidence

When, in one of the jokey moments of the American T.V. show, the NCIS characters reeled off their zodiac signs they were what I had already mentally assigned. Could the fearless, death-dealing, seductive ex-Mossad assassin Ziva be anything but a Scorpio sun – as is the actress herself? Cote d'Pablo, who plays Ziva, has a Leo moon, she belongs in the spotlight. Mark Harmon and his character Gibbs are both workaholic Virgo. In Harmon's case a double Virgo with the sun and moon in the sign and Scorpio rising; so are the producers using astrology in their casting? Virgo is the craftsperson. The actor built his own house, reflecting Gibbs' patient and repetitious boat building, but it is said that despite his busy filming schedule and public persona, the actor maintains as much privacy as possible. Very Scorpio rising, as is the investigative former Marine sniper he plays who gives nothing away and who never forgets. He will exact revenge no matter how long he may have to wait. And wait he can, patiently for days or weeks on end if necessary. Fans of the show will know what happened to the man who killed Gibbs' wife and daughter – revenge, murder and death feature large in the lives of many with Scorpio strong in their birthcharts. But this Virgo character is also dedicated to examining every aspect, leaving no stone unturned until he finds truth and justice – and of course there is the uniform. Virgo does so love a uniform. Even when in 'civvies' Gibbs retains the Marine haircut and *looks* like he's wearing a uniform. But he has a soft heart hidden under that tough outer shell and I'd mentally allocated a Cancer moon to this character who, deprived of his wife and daughter, took on his team as a substitute family but keeps his emotions tightly hidden under an armoured shell.

Or maybe it's the NCIS scriptwriters who draw on astrological characters? Think about Abbey Shuto, the wacky goth who works in the basement. A brilliant forensic scientist who sleeps in a coffin. She has to have a rich seam of Scorpio within her for her intuitive and yet highly technical investigations into the subtle physical evidence surrounding the dead. But what about her soft heart and affinity with nuns, Pisces moon I would think. That wacky exterior has to be Aquarius as does the exacting scientist it hides. And how about Dr 'Ducky' Mallard, the cultured forensic pathologist with a psychology degree? He must also have a strong dose of Scorpio surely? But his sensitive way of talking to the bodies and gently revealing their secrets suggests perhaps there's some Cancer in there – particularly as he lived with his elderly mother virtually up to her death. Despite his shrewdness on occasions (Cancer), he can also be taken in by women, which suggests Pisces as does his occasional ability to see the dead, so perhaps his sun, moon and rising sign form a watery trine around the chart.

I don't recall that Abbey or Ducky were there when the characters called out their zodiac signs, but Tony was.

I'd always attributed an Aries sun to 'very special agent' Anthony Di Nozzo, so much of whose macho character is never-theless a me-orientated vulnerable small boy who is taking an exceedingly long time to grow up. He's certainly got Aries courage. He fearlessly rushes in where fools dare not tread, and he so wants to be the leader – and a babe-magnet. And who else but an Aries would have his heart so set on a red Ferrari? To the best of my memory, which may of course have heard what it expected to hear, he was Aries in the script. Given his obsession with films, Pisces probably features in his chart – which his chaotic romantic life would support. He endlessly chases women, almost immediately letting them down, and yet lost his heart to the one he could never have while working undercover so shall we say a Pisces Moon? The actor himself has a chameleon-like Cancer sun and an adventurous, answer-seeking Sagittarius moon that facilitates playing this surprisingly bright and yet sometimes naïve ex-cop who hated being confined to a ship at sea, much preferring the freedom of his urban environment. I would certainly assign Gemini rising to his character with his love of verbal word play and puns – and an ability to switch his opinions at a tap of the head. His obsession with ferreting out his colleagues' secrets is Gemini too as is his clever interrogation technique.

And what about the main target of his verbal fencing, McGeek as Tony likes to call him? What sign would you give to a nerdy computer genius who can write a best selling thriller and keep his love affairs so well hidden from his obsessively nosy work colleague? Could be technologically savvy Aquarius, of course but he'd need a sensible rising sign to keep him so focused in the here and now. Even though a writer, he's far too good at keeping secrets to be a Gemini. He's a neat-freak so some Virgo in there possibly? But the actor himself is yet another Scorpio, this time with a Capricorn moon – absolutely perfect for a guy who is the son-in-law of a producer of the show. Capricorn is just brilliant at using its contacts to get ahead. But after reading this book perhaps you'll assign a sun, moon and rising sign to his character yourself.

Who dun what? That is the question!

I only want a little bit of butter for my bread.
When we were very young A.A. Milne (Capricorn sun and moon)

This example of astro-characterisation in action is based on an idea suggested by an actual event, one which could become a Midsummer Murders plot or a murder mystery novel depending who in my writing group gets there first. Rumours and conspiracy theories abound as to what actually happened and, as writers will, we have speculated and expanded exponentially on the possible scenarios. It's not so much a case of 'Who Dun It?' as 'Was it done at all?' I'm not suggesting for a moment that there is anything untoward in the original event, only using it to illustrate that everything that happens is fodder to the writer's pen and can be played with, expanded upon and taken way beyond what *was* into a plot, especially if you use the astrology to develop characters that drive it forward and who have enough complexity to allow for several possibilities, or none at all, to be going on at once. The extract that follows the character sketches is from a first draft, drawn to give a sense of the characters and their interaction rather than a taut telling of the tale. The writing needs tightening and you'll have an opportunity to do that, rewriting it yourself based on the impression you gain of the characters.

The Protagonists:

Michael Cozens. Estate agent, community activist and general do-gooder. He recently contacted an old friend offering to hold her Power of Attorney and take care of her financial affairs. But does he have a hidden agenda? He has two daughters who need to fund university educations and a son living in Central America who can't afford to come home. Estate agencies are not doing well in the current economic recession. Has he bitten off more than he thought? His old friend, who is very demanding, loves men especially a charming one with wide, innocent eyes such as he has. He's been called in at all hours of the day and night for the smallest of tasks.

The astrological personality: Mike has his sun in Pisces, the moon in Scorpio and Libra rising. His façade is charming and helpful, a people pleaser – on the surface. People say of him 'what a nice man, you couldn't find anyone better to help you'. His do-gooder sun in Pisces wants to be the rescuer, the saviour, but may have a guilty secret and will almost certainly have an escape route planned. But what about that secretive Scorpio moon? It's much more intense, likely to have a hidden agenda, to look out for number one, to sting without reason. It revels in power, especially power over others too weak to care for themselves. It plots and bewitches its way to victory without giving anything away on the surface. What you see is definitely not what you get with this charmer. Will he be a victim or the perpetrator of a deception? It could go either way.

The name: Michael, the great protector archangel who watches over souls in need. He's the patron saint of grocers and mariners. Pronounced 'cousins' with all that that implies, Cozens means to con or deceive.

Jill Cozens. A former nurse who now helps her husband run his estate agency and looks after all the lame ducks he takes on. Deeply involved with her family, she follows where he leads – most of the time. Jill willingly joins Mike in his get rich quick schemes but there comes a point where she stops to question, something he rarely does.

The astrological personality: Sun in Gemini, moon in Leo and Virgo rising. Virgo rising is finicky and hardworking, offering service or getting stuck in a role of servitude. This detail-orientated rising sign harmonises well with communicative Gemini, which never stops talking and switches viewpoint from moment to moment. Jill never uses one word where ten will do. Nothing will stay the same with this character for long and little that's said will be the whole truth and nothing but the truth. It will be an expedient truth but not a malicious one. But let's think about that superior Leo moon for a moment. It's very proud but also open hearted. It genuinely wants what's best for someone else – until it has to play second fiddle or is found lacking in some way. Then there's a major rethink.

The name: Jill means child of the gods. Jack and Jill went up the hill, Jack fell down and broke his crown, and Jill came tumbling after. Enough said?

Josephine Janine. Former next-door neighbour of the Cozens. Now in her mid-eighties, Josephine has lived as an ex-pat all over the world and has a history of being taken in by men but she's had an extremely good time along the way. She doesn't rate women very highly. She's had four husbands, numerous lovers and many pets, and has now been diagnosed with early dementia due to severe but intermittent short term memory loss. She has no living relatives. She still appears bright as a button and very sociable – from moment to moment. Her credo is 'never turn down an invitation because you don't know where it will lead.' However, these days she often forgets not only the location but the invitation itself.

The astrological personality: With her sun in Libra, moon in Pisces and Sagittarius rising Josephine is game for anything but oh so open to duplicity and guile. She's always looking for the next adventure (Sag), takes people at their face value especially on their looks (Libra/Pisces) and rarely thinks about their depths until she gets sucked down into them. She feels better when she's part of a whole (Libra/Pisces). She drinks, smokes and engages in every kind of escapist fantasy (Pisces). She's been a playwright and a poet since she was a child. But she's got a deep layer of guilt (that moon in Pisces). Her darkest secret is that she blames herself for the fact that she miscarried several times. She believes that she must have done something terribly wrong to be so punished. She would love to have been a mother. That at least two of the miscarriages were due to abuse by her husbands does not seem to her a valid reason, it must have been something *she* did. This could perhaps be traced back to her aristocratic sailor father leaving when she was very young. On the one occasion she did spot him later, she called out to him but he ran away. Ever since she has been seeking a handsome man to love and redeem her. Alas, what she found were loveable rogues and insincere deceivers.

The name: Josephine and Janine were exotic dancers, one hiding behind a fan, and dancing features hugely in Josephine's backstory, which we're not going into here (but you could have fun constructing it for yourself). In Hebrew Josephine means 'God enlarges' or 'he multiplies' and this is a larger than life character but the meaning of Janine 'God is gracious' also holds good. This is a very gracious lady.

The plot:

An elderly lady is approached by two ex-neighbours with whom she had once been friendly. She hasn't seen them since they moved away some years ago but they suddenly call in 'to see how she is and if she needs help?' having heard rumours in the small town in which they all still live that she is failing to cope. She signs a power of attorney that gives them total control over her finances and her person, and a Will that appoints them her executors, and leaves her residuary estate to them. She is taken by them to a new solicitor to make this Will, someone who has no idea that she was a prolific playwright in the past. One of her plays is in course of production and could yield a substantial sum of money. What the executors don't know is that the elderly lady has made several draw-downs on her property and, therefore, has very little equity and minimal liquid assets. They do, however, know that she has a painting on a wooden panel that she was given for her eighteenth birthday when she lived in the South Seas in the 1940s and which is reputed to have been produced by the French artist Gauguin when he lived in the islands. If this can be authenticated it would be worth hundreds of thousands of pounds. They obtain the painting under the ruse of having it valued and hide it in a tin box in the garden of her home. Josephine forgets she has given it to them and tells everyone she has lost it. The 'Power of Attorneys', who will become the executors, want to visit their son who lives in South America.

We join the plot at the point where Josephine has returned home from a Galapagos cruise (she'd been there two years before but said it was a part of the world she hadn't seen). The cruise had been booked by her 'PoAs' who said that she had a bit too much money in the bank so might as well use some of it to enjoy herself. The 'PoAs' told friends who enquired how an elderly lady with severe short term memory loss could possibly cope on such a long distance cruise 'oh there are facilities.' The cruise cost over £5000, which has set the friends wondering and questions are being asked about Josephine's future care and her need for a nursing home, which will be costly. A producer has been found for a play that Josephine had been working on before the dementia set in but the 'PoAs' have failed to communicate with him despite repeated attempts at contact and Josephine can no longer retain the context of his calls. On her return from the cruise, Josephine is taken ill.

Extract from the first draft

'Mike, I'm really worried about Josephine. Her colour is so poor and she can't even walk to the commode with help. She's been throwing up so much I think she must have Norovirus. It's doing the rounds especially on those cruise ships. We'd better get her to hospital.' Jill brushes back the still-dark hair from the pale sweaty face in front of her. Josephine responds by throwing up yet again and Jill quickly wipes away the slime that's all that's left in the heaving stomach. She rolls her sleeve up with her finger tips, nose wrinkling at the smell. 'Here, try to sip some water,' she coaxes but Josephine shakes her head.

'Gin,' she demands. 'That'll get me better. And a fag.'

'What are you like?' sighs Jill. 'Mike, we have to get her some proper care, she's so dehydrated. Look at her, the poor thing can barely move, see how she's trembling, and her skin – oops, there you go dear, managed to catch that bit. Let's just wipe your face. Mike we must ... '

'Nonsense, you were a nurse weren't you. You can take care of her. She'll only pick up some other bug in hospital and we don't want her to have to go into a care home. You don't want to go to hospital do you Josephine?' He articulates the words carefully, as though speaking to a child.

'Wh ... what? Hospital? Why? I'm not ill ... am I?'

Jill has to bend her head close to Josephine's mouth to make out the words, but doesn't get too close, she's wary of being vomited on again. Desperate to wash her sleeve, she dabs at it once more with the cloth. 'Yes dear, you are, you've been throwing up all week. You haven't moved off that sofa. You need to be in hospital.'

'Where's the dog? ... Where's my Mitzie?'

'Don't you remember dear, when you couldn't walk her anymore you gave her to that nice family over Southampton way?' Jill tries again to brush the sweaty hair away to the side. Josephine took such pride in her appearance, how can she have got like this?

'I never did. I'd never give away my Mitzie.' The sunken eyes roam round the room, staring at the empty lead hanging on the door. 'I want Mitzie. She's my friend. Like you Mike'. It's a wail, although a quiet one.

'I'm afraid you did Josephine. You should never have had another after Hero died. You knew you couldn't rely on finding someone else to walk her. It was too much for me, I spend so much time doing things for other people. That takes up all my energy. I've no time for walks.' Mike turns to leave. 'Jill, you're in charge. Is there anything you need?'

'Some rehydrate might help, and chicken soup. There's a pot

in the fridge at home that you made a day or two ago, could you bring that?'

'There's some in Josephine's fridge I bought it in that day for her, use that. I don't think she's touched it today.'

'Well, she can't stand so I doubt she went in there to get it. But I think I need the rehydrate, now.'

'Yes, yes, I'll need to call into the agency first, make sure the girls are on top of things. I'll be back within the hour. Now you take care of yourself Josephine.' As he pats her thin shoulder Josephine beams up at him adoringly.

'Anything you say handsome. Don't go, stay and look after me. She can sort out the girls ... '

'That rehydrate's urgent. Couldn't you come straight ... '

Too late, the front door has closed behind him. Jill hadn't even noticed him getting his coat. She makes her way to the kitchen at the back of the house. When she opens the fridge door she recoils in disgust. Sitting in solitary splendour is a half full bowl of scummy soup: greasy-topped, faintly green, but still soup. She recognises the bowl as one of her own. Surely this can't be what Mike meant, this can't be what he's been feeding Josephine on? This hasn't been here a day or two. It can't have been. It's too old, surely ... And what about that Campylobacter thingie, is that what Josephine's suffering from? The man from the Foods Standard Agency said on the radio that two-thirds of chickens were infected. People have died from it. He said not to wash chicken because it spreads the bacteria but she always does, and pats it dry with a paper towel. What did Mike do, could the chicken have been infected, is that why the soup's gone that phosphorescent green? We really do need to get her to hospital. What will people think? They won't blame us, will they, she asks herself. Just in case, she tips the soup down the sink, boils a kettle and washes out the bowl. To be completely sure she scrubs out the fridge as well, switches it off and leaves the door open for it to air. If only there was some antibacterial cleaner in the house.

Three hours later Jill is distracted from her book by a faint groan from the sofa.

'What is it dear, what can I do for you?'

'My picture, my birthday picture, where is it? Mike said he'd take it to London for me, get it authenticated, it was given to me for my birthday you know,' her hand is groping beneath the stained cushions, 'the man said it came from Gauguin, he painted it, it was my ticket out of there, not that I particularly wanted to leave, I loved those islands, and the purser on the inter-island steamer, he was gorgeous, I nearly married him you know and Bertie from Burns Philp, but ... ' she struggles to sit up but falls back exhausted.

'Quietly Josephine, you'll tire yourself. I'm sure it's safe, don't try to talk.' What can she say? She knows Mike buried the picture in a box in the back garden while Josephine was off on her trip. She'd been worried that Josephine might wander off while in port – if she ever made it past the airport that is – but he'd laughed it off. She's been travelling the world since she was four he'd said, no reason to stop now. At least it gave them a break from her constant phone calls, she'd never realised before just how needy Josephine was. They had time to be a couple again, when she wasn't chasing after his other lame ducks or organising lifts for the girls. Thank god Josephine had given them her old car that had really helped. When she'd protested about the picture getting damaged Mike had assured her it was well wrapped and safe.

'No point in having it authenticated now,' he'd said, 'it'll only add to the value of the estate. Best to find it later, after she's gone. If anyone finds out they'll think she hid it. As it stands now we can probate the Will ourselves and that'll be a lot less hassle – and cheaper – than getting solicitors involved. We deserve it after all we've done for her.'

Jill had agreed at the time, after all they were the residuary beneficiaries as well as the executors of the new Will he'd persuaded Josephine to sign before she left for her trip. With luck there'd be enough for their girls to come out of uni with no debts, and a bit left over for a treat. That visit they'd promised themselves to Guatemala to see Corin, they could do that ... once she'd gone. Even bring him back with them if he wanted to come home. But she'll miss her. Miss those mischievous eyes and the cloud of smoke that announced her presence. Just as she'd missed the parties once they'd moved to the other side of town. She'd thought it would be good to get away as Josephine had always wanted to know what they were up to. But it left a hole. What fun they used to have, what stories she'd told of her travels. Why didn't they keep up the friendship? What made ... and why has Josephine remembered that Mike had the painting, she'd forgotten that when she last asked where it was. Told everyone she'd lost it. She glances warily at her old friend.

Josephine has gone very quiet, her face the colour of the putty round the ancient windows and her breath less than the draught that comes through the ill-fitting door. A shining snail's trail of drool creeps down her chin. Jill shakes her gently, 'Come on old thing, wake up.' But there is only silence.

'Yes, an ambulance please, immediately ... How long? ... No sooner than that? OK, I'll try to keep her going, but please hurry.' Jill turns back to Josephine forcing water between the tightly pursed lips that used to pucker with air-blown kisses and constant laughter. It dribbles out again, washing away the drool. 'They're coming, it won't be long now. We'll have you in hospital soon as look at you ... '

'What, did you phone for an ambulance? How are we going to explain this? What have you done? She'll definitely need a nursing home now if she isn't dead already. They're bound to blame us.'

It's Mike. He's back.

'Come on quickly, sit her up and make it look like it's just happened. They won't ask too many questions ...'

'But …'

'No buts, you've been alone with her all day, it'll be your fault. You'd better have your story ready for when the police come calling.'

The extract is, as I said, from a first draft that fleshes out the characters and the way they interact from the astrology. I'd cut it down drastically on the second edit but it gives me a sense that fastidious Gemini-Virgo Jill talks constantly, to herself if there's no one else to listen, and that she notices every little detail. That she's torn between her desire to please her husband and a need to look after her old friend and, in the end, does the right thing as she sees it (Leo moon). That Josephine has memory loss, yes, but she still loves the attention of a charming man (Pisces-Libra). And the man himself? Do you get a sense of Piscean slipperiness, can you pin him down? Did he or did he not take advantage of a vulnerable old lady (Scorpio) or was he being sincere and doing what he thought best for her (Libra)?

- Rewrite the story yourself and create your own ending using the astrological characteristics and what you've already learned from the protagonists to drive the story forward.

Chapter 3

Getting started

August 23rd, 2011

There's very little that can beat the buzz of starting work on a new book. I'm not talking about the mental preparation, the character breakdowns, the background searches, the frenetic visualisation – all of which put the fear of God into me. No, it's the actual writing that is so compulsive. The 'not knowing where you're about to go' feeling one gets when starting on a new chapter. The quasi osmotic creation of character beneath your very eyes, when the way you thought it would go isn't the way it goes at all. I call it 'living on the hoof'. You start off by thinking you're in charge, but you soon realise that the story is in charge of you. That you are drawing from wells you didn't even know existed. *http://blog.marioreading.com* Mario Reading (Leo sun and moon Libra rising)

So, by now you will have grasped the idea and be all set to create those astro-characters.

- Read through the description of each zodiac sign and select the one that best fits the character you have in mind. Pick a birth date within the timeframe of that sign.
- Then chose a moon-sign that will create the kind of emotional tensions, undercurrents, old tapes, secrets desires and needs that you wish to portray.
- Mask it all with a rising sign that offers a smokescreen for your reader to penetrate.
- Interview your character (see Chapter 4) and create a profile.

Think about specific characteristics and actions – describing your character flicking dandruff off the collar of a man she has just met for instance conveys far more than merely saying she is finicky about personal grooming. (If she does that, she's probably a sun in Virgo or has Virgo-rising but she will undoubtedly have an assertive sun or rising-sign.)

To help you create, you can interview your character as this will often surprise you and unfold what is waiting in the zeitgeist to make itself known in your story.

To practice:

- Write a character profile to fit a potential storyline.

- Or, to challenge yourself and explore the concept further, open the book at random three times and create a character profile and short story based on the sun, moon and rising signs that chance reveals.

Don't forget that your character will need to develop and grow throughout the book so hold something in reserve, don't reveal everything at once!

Character check list

- Each character needs to be recognisably different, intriguing and surprising.
- Names are important – make them relevant to time and setting.
- Place your character in a setting where he or she can interact with others and/or with the environment.
- Reveal, don't tell, what drives a character.
- Leave visual descriptions loose for the reader to flesh out, with one memorable feature, but use plenty of dialogue and characteristic actions.

- Give your protagonist attitude.
- Each character needs a conflict, dilemma or challenge to solve.
- Introduce the protagonist at a point of life change, show how the character develops as the plot unfolds.
- Give your character a dominant trait – motherliness, appeasement, always on the pull, etc. Think emotions, beliefs, hang-ups, phobias – relate these to the sun-moon-rising signs you choose.
- Give your protagonist a deep dark secret and plenty of emotional baggage even if you never share this with your reader.
- Body language: He or she looks like a person who would...
- Verbal language: He or she speaks like a person who ...
- Senses: He or she smells like ...
- A character tag – e.g. wears a particular brand, reads a magazine backwards, drinks a specific wine/herb tea/black coffee, or has a wonky eye is useful.
- Give your character a close friend and let the friend unfold the character and their relationship to the reader.
- By the end of the story your protagonist should have changed markedly.
- Avoid implausible or shallow characters even minor ones. If they deserve to be in the story, they need to shine as a character in their own right.

Chapter 4

Interview your character

Don't clamor for an interview. Instead search for the INNER VIEW.

Sri Sathya Sai Baba (Scorpio sun, Cancer moon, Scorpio rising)

You need to know your character inside out and backwards but then be prepared to be surprised. Let your character grow and develop organically. Every author has had the experience of a character taking over and developing themselves, minor characters sometimes become the core of a book and all protagonists, just as with real people, do something completely out of character now and then. Interviewing your character helps you to be ready for the surprises. But you'll find the reason lies in that interplay of sun, moon and rising sign. To assist, here's a list of questions to get you started, some of them are deliberately repetitious, others you could ask twice and get a different answer on each day. Try it and see:

Name:
Address:
Sun-sign:
Key points:
Moon-sign:
Key points:
Rising-sign:
Key points:
Surroundings?
Occupation?
Age?

Marital status?
Family?
Appearance?
Favourite item of clothing?
Favourite colour?
How does your character smell?
Voice and verbal style?
Most used word or phrase?
Lifestyle?
Favourite food?
How does your character eat?
How does your character approach life?
How does your character interact with people?
Hobbies?
Reads/watches?
Where does your character go on holiday?
Husband/wife/lover/partner/secret liaison?
Best friend?
What habits and tendencies does your character have?
What's the most irritating thing about your character?
What would your character never do?
Earliest memory:
Smell?
Sight?
Sound?
Touch?
Feeling?
Worst memory?
Favourite memory?
Did your character always have his or her needs met?
Does he or she have them met now?
What unmet needs does your character have?
Most surprising fact?
Is your character sociable?

Background:

Ten key facts:

Ten key events:

Ten key people:

Deepest secret?

Would your character choose to lie if it was easier than telling the truth?

Passionate about?

Abhors?

Gets angry about?

Fears?

Biggest conflict, challenge or dilemma?

Two idiosyncrasies:

Six character traits:

Does your character express feelings easily?

What is your character's greatest joy?

What is your character's greatest stress?

How does your character react to stress?

How does your character react to someone else's pain?

Pet hate?

How does the public face differ from the private?

What would your character like to change about his or her life?

What would he or she change about him or herself?

What dreams did your character have that have flown away?

What does your character hope for?

How does your character feel about death?

What does your character want you to know?

What does your character not want you to know?

What does your character never reveal to anyone?

Where does your character go to get away from it all?

Sum up your character's personality in three words:

Close your eyes and see if your character has anything else to say:

Chapter 5

P.S. Zodiac Sex Style

Ok, let's face it. No matter what kind of story you are writing, your protagonist will have sex on his or her mind at some point in the story. Not every tale is a love story but all your characters' relationships will be coloured by the zodiac signs you've chosen. Each sign has a distinctive approach to love, friendship, family, co-workers and close relationships – which is set out in the profiles that follow. But first here's a quick and dirty guide that skims the surface but which instantly gives an idea of which sun-sign you could choose for your character and how selecting a clashing moon and rising sign add interest, internal struggle and a dash of the unexpected to the mix. Choosing a sign with clashing tendencies for a partner, friend or co-worker would add another layer of tension to your plot:

Aries:
Style: Active. Raunchy. Impatient. Too fast? Too bad!
Says: "Me first".
Prelims: Doesn't bother
Enjoys: Danger
Relationship quality: Selfish
Achilles heel: Impatient for new experiences

Taurus:
Style: Passive. Sensual. Savours slowly. Can be boring.
Says: "Let's get comfortable"
Prelims: A good meal
Enjoys: Massage
Relationship quality: Loyal
Achilles heel: Too entrenched

Gemini:

Style: Active. Eloquent. Sex occurs mostly in the head. Talks continuously.
Says: "Do you think ...."
Prelims: A good conversation
Enjoys: Talking through the Kama Sutra
Relationship quality: Changeable
Achilles heel: Naivety

Cancer:

Style: Passive. Possessive. Cuddlesome. Caring. Emotional.
Says: "I'll look after you."
Prelims: Cooking for two
Enjoys: A quiet evening in
Relationship quality: Clingy.
Achilles heel: Neediness

Leo:

Style: Active. Lustful. Romantic. Larger than life. Egocentric.
Says: "Do I look good in this?"
Prelims: Flattery
Enjoys: A good evening out
Relationship quality: Narcissistic
Achilles heel: Pride

Virgo:

Style: Passive. Discerning. Earthy sensuality. Cool ardour. Analytical.
Says: "I'll just freshen up first ... "
Prelims: Checking how tidy the bedroom is
Enjoys: Perfection
Relationship quality: Picky
Achilles heel: Dirt

Libra:

Style: Passive. Alluring. Amorous. Accommodating. Partner-centred.

Says: "What would please you?"

Prelims: Being courted and flattered

Enjoys: Harmony

Relationship quality: Adaptive

Achilles heel: People-pleasing

Scorpio:

Style: Active. Magnetic. Intense. Secretive. Jealous.

Says: "Tell me all about yourself."

Prelims: Beautiful underwear

Enjoys: Bondage, allure, mystery

Relationship quality: Ouch!

Achilles heel: Secrets and lies

Sagittarius:

Style: Active. Adventurous. Easily bored. The grass is greener elsewhere.

Says: "Excuse me, I'll be right back."

Prelims: A plane ticket

Enjoys: New experiences

Relationship quality: Freedom

Achilles heel: Promises too much

Capricorn:

Style: Active. Cautious. Reserved. Surprisingly highly sexed.

Says: "Are you serious?"

Prelims: Checking the bank balance

Enjoys: Quality above quantity

Relationship quality: Committed

Achilles heel: Keeping up appearances

Aquarius:

Style: Active. Detached. Inventive. Electric. A real one-off
Says: "Have you tried … ?"
Prelims: Friendship
Enjoys: The weird and wacky
Relationship quality: Dispassionate
Achilles heel: Throwing the baby out with the bathwater.

Pisces:

Style: Passive. Romantic. In love with love. Rose tinted glasses. Swims off.
Says: "I've finally found what I've been searching for"
Prelims: Declaration of undying love.
Enjoys: Fantasy and variety
Relationship quality: Serial soulmates
Achilles heel: Sucker for a sob-story

Chapter 6

Aries
The Ram

♈ **21 March - 19 April**

She was an Amazon. Her whole life was spent riding at breakneck speed along the wilder shores of love.
The Wilder Shores of Love Lesley Blanch (Gemini sun, Pisces moon)

Crib sheet

First impression: Rambunctious and assured. Loud and pushy.

Appearance: Bold 'ram's-horn' eyebrows meet in the middle below a strong forehead. Widow's peak. Red tinge to hair is common.

Stance: Energetic, athletic, cocky, confrontational and confident.

Dress: Wears bright, dramatic clothes. Favours red or black. 'Power dresses' or wears casual clothes.

Favourite word: I.

Says: Me first. I'll do it. I think you'll find I'm right. Let's …

Never says: Sorry. After you.

Career: Army, wheeler-dealer, surgeon, truck driver, entrepreneur, C.E.O., self employed or the innovative boss with a good support team, politician.

Archetype: The hero.

Shadow: The procrastinator.

Likes: Excitement. Risk. Competitive or dangerous sports. Adventure and frenetic activity. Fast cars. Social whirl. Metalwork.

Dislikes: Monotony. Teamwork. Hypocrisy. Injustice. Taking orders. Inactivity. Hates being in the wrong.

Money: Spends freely.

Dreams: Of a more honourable world.

Getting to know Aries

Style: Bold, impulsive, independent and assertive, pushy and difficult to ignore. A born leader.

A knight on a white charger dashing to the rescue, with me what you see is what you get. I am not a subtle sign. I never suffer fools – or boredom – gladly. First impressions count with me. I know my own mind, I take to people or I don't, there is no neutral ground. Quick to anger, I have rapid powers of recovery and don't hold a grudge. I'm a born leader who enjoys a challenge. I'm naturally competitive and quick. I like action and I have immense courage. You'll find me frank, open and headstrong. Some people call me gung-ho but I prefer to think of myself as a courageous initiator and pioneer. I like to fight for the underdog. I prefer to delegate the grunt work and to let someone else do the follow-up. I've got strong needs and I don't hesitate to make them known. Other people accuse me of being insensitive and say my interaction with others is naïve and self-centred. That doesn't bother me.

What Makes Aries Tick: I'm transparent. I don't have the guile –

or the patience – to manipulate and manoeuvre and I can't stand people who do. It's simple. I'm exuberant and straightforward and I simply go all out for what I want. I like my needs gratified instantly and make my views known forcefully. Other people call my reaction when I don't get my own way a tantrum. But I can't stand frustration so playing a waiting game is not on. I need action and I want to be upfront and honest. It's natural for me to be the leader in any undertaking because I'm always right and I have good reasons for my actions no matter how quickly the decision was made. I have a great desire to fight for the underdog and to right wrongs – although I've been accused of tilting at windmills. I really enjoy a good challenge – or a fight.

The Aries shadow: Me have flaws? No way! Quirks, maybe. I've been accused of having an overwhelming ego, procrastination, a tendency to vacillate or be manipulative and economical with the truth when expedient but that's just bullshit. I've been told I lack perseverance and am exceedingly selfish. I simply walk away. Well, I might shout a bit first or even get violent. I do have a quick temper and a tendency to lash out but it's over and done with quickly and if I can forget, why can't others? People get upset when I abandon them without warning. I can't think why. I'm done with them. I have contempt for those beneath me but sometimes, to my surprise, I am unable to say no and have difficulty in delivering what is promised but people shouldn't expect me to. In my other life I'm a dark knight who is the mercenary or the gun-runner, the take-over-and-sell-out-shark, or the legal conniver.

Aries speak: 'Loved the soldier reference. How's that for an Aries South Node soul with Mars there? Turning around the warrior energy to heal now. Right there by your side, congratulations on getting through your first treatment, my brave spiritual soldier!' Neil. *Under cover of Darkness* blog comment (http://wwww.

margaretcahill.wordpress.com/).

Your Aries male character

I write my own script. I'm the original macho man, the most immediate and primal expression of masculinity. My rambunctiousness is infinitely superior to the other males in the zodiac and I'll fight anyone who says different. It gives me great pleasure to protect my woman and those lesser mortals below me. Highly competitive, I'm always going to be on top. I go all out for what I want. I'm active and volatile, as easily roused to anger as to passion. There's nothing cool or laid back about me. I freely admit I want to dominate and make my mark on the world: fast. Don't expect me to show patience or to understand nuances and subtleties. I act on my instincts, spontaneously without pause for thought, and I'm intensely involved in the business of living. I lead from way out front to satisfy my craving for adventure. Somewhat reluctantly, I learn through experiences as I already know everything there is to know. Woe betide you if you try to give me directions or put me straight. I hate to be told I've made a mistake or that I've failed. It's always someone else's fault. If anyone tries to say different there'll be fireworks. Praise me, flatter me, let me have my way and we'll get on fine. There are times when I test your tolerance, and your ability to forgive, to the limits but no one is going to forget me in a hurry.

Your Aries female character

Like my male counterpart, I'm feisty, active, spontaneous and macho. I'm going to tell you exactly how I want to be portrayed. Nothing wimpish or frilly for me. I have no truck with feminine wiles and get my way through direct confrontation and inspired leadership. People say I'm a dominant woman who knows what she wants and goes all out to get it. Yes I do. But I think you'll find I also have a charming quality of naïve innocence when it suits me. Pushy as I might be, you'll find it impossible to be angry with bodacious me for long. But I'm not unfeminine. I like to be wooed and relish romantic gestures such as the presentation of a single red rose – and not only from my lover. I'm just as up front about my sexual needs and lusts as the male ram. If you let me take the lead, I reward you with undying devotion. Try to take charge of me and I'll dump you in disgust.

Aries in love

Love style: Passionate, romantic, impetuous, reasonably faithful. Emotionally headstrong.

I'm independent. I'm not someone else's other half. Partnership is not a state that comes naturally to me and I find it difficult to adjust to other people's needs especially if they don't make these immediately apparent. I can't be doing with heavy hints and lethal silences. I find it hard to distinguish between love and desire. I quickly fall head over heels in lust, and sometimes into marriage as well. But the desire can pass just as quickly. I'm one of the zodiac's raunchiest signs. My libido runs high and I thoroughly enjoy sexual conquest. Some people say I'm rapacious. I prefer to say I have passionate encounters and dynamite sex. I like to make the running and rarely take no for an answer. If someone really isn't interested, I quickly move on. Why waste time? But I'm a romantic at heart. I enjoy the rituals of courtship: the flowers, the presents, and the intimate dinners *a deux* – but no emotional games thank you. I let other signs play those.

Aries seeks: short, sharp sex; love, lifelong lust, romance and adventure, faithfulness, challenge and a degree of commitment.

Seduction technique: I'm intensely passionate, brash, blatant, and totally honest. Why be anything else? I want to conquer and get it on without delay. I don't wait to be asked. I'm sexually provocative, impatient and pushy and it works for me.

Flirting: I love to flirt and if my partner's wise I'll get plenty of leeway because in all probability I'll go home with the person I arrived with. But not always!

Trust and Intimacy: I'm terribly naïve and I find this challenging.

Secret Sexual Desire: Submissive sex with a stranger.

Aries as a Partner

Partnership style: pushy, dominant, macho, romantic.

I can behave romantically, showering my partner with gifts and, occasionally, expressing my feelings with flowery sentiment; but, so past partners have told me, I can also behave with great selfishness and be utterly insensitive and inconsiderate. To be honest, I find the whole notion of equal partnership problematic, preferring to dominate a situation. There are times when I simply go ahead and do what I know is right without consulting my partner. I'm always surprised when this leads to friction. I know what's best after all. I'll let you into a secret. In my heart I'm seeking a soulmate, a life partner, and if someone comes close to the ideal, or appears to, I rush into matrimony. Once there, the flaws may rapidly become apparent but I continue to hope, although I have to admit I'm not the most faithful person in the world. My need for fast sex and constant stimulation may lead to brief affairs. It doesn't hurt anyone does it? I don't feel disloyal when indulging in a one night stand – or even when conducting a friendship with benefits for that matter. But I'm not so forgiving if my partner strays. I'm not jealous, but I am hot blooded and I need to come first. I don't want my partner sharing amorous glances or anything else with anyone but me thank you very much.

What Aries expects from a partner: I expect unswerving loyalty and total attention. My partner won't have time for anyone else and they won't need a life outside the relationship. My partner has accused me of having a box in which they're parked until I'm ready to take them out to play – or to mate. Bollocks to that!

When a relationship ends: Past relationships have ended with me storming out. I didn't intend to stay gone. Like my ardour, my anger is easily aroused but cools just as quickly. I expect my partner to know that. Rather than saying 'sorry', I like to have sex to make up. But some partners haven't stayed around long enough to find that out. Once final parting has occurred however, I put the relationship out of my mind and get on with life as quickly as possible. I'll soon find a replacement.

Aries as a friend

Friendship style: straightforward, dominant, exciting.

I am an extremely straightforward sign. Which means I'm honest, faithful and, I don't mind telling you, opinionated. An adrenaline junkie, I expect friends to keep up with a multitude of activities, many of them sports based and almost all carrying danger to life and limb. Your character and I will have an active social life together but this is not an exclusive relationship. We'll try out new adventures. There'll be invitations to all the latest health kicks and no one is more supportive when starting a diet or new hobby – or quicker to urge letting it go. What the hell, life's too short? Mind you, I want to be leader of the pack and provided I'm not coerced, I can be flexible – for a time. If I like new options, I adopt them as my own, or find something more stimulating.

People don't understand my fiery temper and low boredom threshold. I love to argue for the sake of arguing. I get off on challenge and conflict. So I'm not the best friend for a character who values peace and quiet as it leads to tension – for them. I just move on. But if your character enjoys a challenge, debates and argues with vigour and is up for an adventure I'm a happy ram. Everyone has a right to their own opinion, even if they are wrong, so there is no comeback if your character has the nerve to disagree with me. In times of crisis I can be called on to help your character fight battles and right wrongs, but I don't have much truck with emotions and find secrets tiresome and impossible to keep.

Aries as a co-worker

Co-worker style: ambitious, independent, pushy, sometimes non-cooperative.

I'm not a team player. Mine is the most independent sign in the zodiac so it's difficult for me to be a co-anything. I want to be boss. I don't do cooperation or talking things through. I lead from the front and I'm brilliant at initiating. It's incredibly tedious to have to carry things through to their conclusion. With me for a co-worker your character will have to pick up the pieces and carry on regardless, I rarely stop to delegate or to explain. But there are advantages. Things have a habit of happening around me and it's never dull. This is where the action is. Promotion is likely too because I give credit where credit is due and co-workers get to share in my glory. On the other hand, if there's a cock up it's their fault. I rarely stay around to share in the blame.

By the light of the full-on moon

Aries moon style: Naïve, child-like. 'Me first, me always'.
Basic drive: expressing urgent ego needs.

I'll happily spoon but we'll do it my way. I have to be the leader. I'll give your character abundant courage and initiative, strong ideals and plenty of stamina. A character with me as the moon is going to be forcefully assertive. I dislike being told what to do, or being given advice, so don't try. And I don't suffer fools gladly. I'm often accused of being selfish and self-centred. People say I'm rather childlike and have tantrums if I don't get my way instantly. They don't realise how overwhelming my needs are. I suppose I am great at throwing my toys out of the pram. I may be headstrong but all I want is to be praised for my courage and individuality. I'm single minded and insensitive yes, but I hate being kept waiting or, even worse, being frustrated. It makes me feel physically ill. Sometimes I hold back from fear of being criticised. Of course, I never do the wrong thing but people sometimes say I do even though it's their fault. Deep down I'm really angry. I don't know where this comes from, I was born like it. I get my nurturing from flattery and respect from other people.

Meeting the world

Aries rising style: up-front and visible.

A natural warrior, when your character puts me on to face the world I'm bold, brash and assertive, determined to be first in everything. You can't miss me. I'm right up there in front putting the world to rights and fighting injustice wherever I meet it. Other people often describe me as 'pushy' but I just want to put my considerable leadership abilities to good use – and to get my own way. War and conflict come naturally to me. Inside your character might be shaking like a jelly but no one will ever know. I can cover up the most insecure of sun-signs and I give the timid and wimpish a bit of a push. I make them look self-confident and capable, although sometimes a bit too selfish. There are times when I could do with a bit of help but I don't know how to ask for it or how to cooperate in joint ventures.

Aries compatibility rating:

Aries***; Taurus *; Gemini ****; Cancer **; Leo *****; Virgo: ***; Libra: *****; Scorpio ***; Sagittarius *****; Capricorn ***; Aquarius **; Pisces *

Chapter 7

Taurus
The Bull

♉ 20 April - 21 May

Is she not pure gold, my mistress?
Robert Browning (Taurus sun, Gemini moon)

Crib sheet

First impression: Solid. Sturdy and trustworthy.

Appearance: Large head on a thick neck above powerful shoulders, body tapers to slender ankles and feet. Or, diminutive size. But always well shaped, melting eyes, broad face and mellifluous voice. Corpulence is common in middle age. The practical exterior hides a hedonistic interior.

Stance: Stocky, stands firmly on the earth. Taurus moves slowly but purposefully and may appear indolent until aroused.

Dress: Wears strong, earthy colours and stylish but comfortable clothes in sensual fabrics.

Favourite Word: Mine.

Says: Forever. Why change? Let's go for quality.

Never says: Let's do something different, I see what you mean, I forgive you.

Career: Banker, singer, musician, artistic, administrator, architect, jeweller, restaurateur, gardener, manager.

Archetype: The conservator.

Shadow: The obstinate bigot.

Likes: Fine things, gourmet food, comfort, opulent surroundings, music and art, wining and dining, sex, gardening, d.i.y., sculpture, art and antique collecting, interior design, contact sports.

Dislikes: Poverty, change, quick decisions.

Money: Money equals security but spends on quality.

Dreams: Of owning the world.

Getting to know Taurus

Style: Stubborn, cautious, tenacious, loyal, steadfast and dependable, materialistic, generous and artistic. A natural supporter.

To be honest I have to admit that I find it difficult to think outside the box. I enjoy routine and I want security and stability. I can withstand great personal misery in order to maintain the status quo. Other people say I'm fixed and inflexible, and warn that I deeply dislike change. I just want things to stay the way they are. They also accuse me of having a strongly possessive nature and a stubborn adherence to duty. I want to see things through and even if I'm a square peg in a round hole I stick it out to the end. Life can become a rut, a grave even. I'm strongly attached to security symbols such as my house, job and marriage, and I find it difficult to see things from another's point of view. I'm very slow to anger but I have a terrible temper when I do blow, and the ability to hold a grudge forever.

What makes Taurus tick: Security is my biggest concern. I want life to be safe, orderly and predictable, and expect promises to be kept. I pride myself on being dependable. I abhor change and need time to adjust – even when it involves something I deeply desire. Gentle coaxing works best with me. The slightest sign of coercion and I refuse to budge even when I know it makes sense. I tread cautiously and make very certain before committing to anything. Emotional introspection does not come easily to me and I find it extremely difficult to discuss intimate feelings or to change ingrained views that are based on past experience. I want to enjoy a comfortable lifestyle. I love luxury and good food. Comfort – and the material trappings of 'the good life' – the house, the car, the married state – mean a great deal to me. They are symbolic of my status. Once I've found these, there is a reluctance to let go and I remain in a situation or relationship long after it has become stultified.

The Taurus shadow: People say that I lack a sense of humour, carry smouldering rage and an inability to look at different points of view. People sometimes call me Tore-ass, I get so mad with them. The ultimate grudge bearer, it's been said that I never forget. They find me a lethal enemy, a bit like a ticking time bomb that's lost its timer and could go off at any moment. I will admit to sometimes being overly self-indulgent, living the ostentatious good life with evangelical fervour and plunging into gluttony and hedonism. A love of fine things makes my darker self the ideal art thief, property wheeler-dealer or financial fraudster.

Taurus speak: 'Why don't I leave him? Well, there's the house. We worked hard for that and I've got it just the way I want it, it's so comfortable. And then there's my job in our company. And we've been together for 35 years. Yes, I know that 34 of them have been unhappy but it's been ok.' [a Taurus client.]

Your male Taurus character

I will reveal myself to you slowly – and consistently. I have few surprises and once established I'm difficult to change. To understand me, you need to know that everything I do is orientated towards my security. I need to feel stable, safe and comfortable. If pushed outside my comfort zone I become stubborn and dogmatic. Faced with inevitable change, I hold it back no matter what the cost to myself or others. Whilst I am superb in a practical crisis, I dislike dramas or tantrums and simply withdraw my attention. In most matters, however, I am supportive, although people have accused me of being bossy as I believe my advice is the most sensible and can't understand why it wouldn't be acted on instantly. Once I am committed to anything, I give my all – and expect the same in return. But you'll have to winkle me out of the rut I've dug myself into. I've been accused of being one of the most jealous and possessive signs of the zodiac. I like to hold onto the things that belong to me. You need to know that a Taurus never forgets – and forgiveness is enormously difficult for me. It also helps you to know that, whilst a generous soul at heart, I like to look after the money. I may spend lavishly on luxury and opulence myself, but I check for quality and good workmanship. I have strong values and know my own mind.

Do not rush me. I like to do things deliberately and to follow my tried and tested routine. When leaving the house I gather everything up, check, and check again. I cannot hurry, nor will I be hurried. If pushed I am an immovable object – or I can explode in a spectacular example of the legendary Taurean rage. Please don't ask me to do two things at once. However, I'll let you into a secret, earthy and practical though I may be, I belong to one of the most sensual and tenacious signs of the zodiac. I may be somewhat lacking in imagination but I have a powerful libido and enormous staying power. I thrive on indolent sensual experiences, both sexual and material. I'm dynamite in bed.

Your female Taurus character

I'm a stubborn, complex mix of materialism, sensuality and pragmatism. I'm excellent at crafts and have many practical skills. My luscious body wears underclothes of silk, and, if necessary, a thick woollen jumper over the top. I value comfort above everything and crave certainty and security. My appetites are large and I have enormous stamina. I offer loyalty and faithfulness and am deeply hurt if these are betrayed. I appreciate quality and always demand the best. Don't, under any circumstances, expect me to rough it. I value comfort highly and I have a certain standard below which I will not go, especially where food or accommodation is concerned. Avoid the fast food outlet and head for a decent restaurant if you want to keep me sweet tempered. Pamper me, never hurry me or give me a cheap present. Even in poverty, I will scour the charity shops for quality items and ensure I never go without. My inner struggle resolves around keeping what I've got and facing up to anything which risks losing that but gives me an opportunity to evolve.

Taurus in love

Love style: loyal and dependable, enjoying old-fashioned romance.

Although I'm initially slow to act, my cool exterior conceals an earthy sexuality – and a deeply jealous nature. I belong to the most sensual sign of the zodiac. My indolent appearance gives little sign of the passionate nature and strong libido that lie quiescent until aroused by carnal desire – when seductiveness oozes out of my every pore. Beauty is a great turn on for me. Sybaritic and pleasure orientated, I indulge every sense, especially taste and smell. I love good food and eating is an essential part of my sexual ritual (body paint was invented by me). My life is not ruled by lust though, I'm too cautious for that and I keep strong control over my urges. I'm concerned with my personal security and won't jeopardise it by acting precipitately.

But when I'm sure, my partner becomes the centre of my world. I want a relationship that lasts for life.

Taurus seeks: security and continuity.

Seduction technique: I'm averse to risk and want sex to be safe and predictable but thoroughly enjoyable so I'm careful in my choices. I love to move in slowly, building up gradually and savouring each moment. But when I turn my magnets on, few can resist. To show my desire I take a prospective partner out on the town, or give an intimate dinner. I like the security of my friends around me for support as I work my slow seduction. I enjoy giving and receiving tangible love tokens.

Flirting: A touchy subject this. I take relationship seriously and prefer one partner for life. My notions of faithfulness exclude flirting, even the most light hearted kind, unless I'm unattached. But my melting eyes and seductive voice can be used to excellent effect and I sometimes forget my principles under the influence of an excellent vino.

Trust and Intimacy: I'm slow to trust, resistant to intimacy.

Secret Sexual Desire: Body piercing.

Taurus as a partner

Partnership style: Because I'm so loyal and faithful, I take it for granted that my partner is too.

I am very partnership orientated but I have been accused of seeing my partner as an extension of myself, a status symbol – the classic trophy wife or husband. I've also been told I take partners for granted, but I'm not being neglectful. I tend to overlook the small courtesies of everyday loving attention forgetting that other people need that. I like to have allocated nights for sex and anything different throws me out of my routine. I'm not really one for spontaneous sexual encounters. To be honest, I don't feel the need to work on my relationship and I may not notice that my partner is bored and in need of something new. Someone trying to move in and take my partner over really rattles my cage though. Nothing rouses my temper more than jealousy. And I rarely forget an indiscretion. Forgiveness is definitely not my strong suit.

What Taurus expects from partners: Absolute integrity and faithfulness is essential for me. I must be able to trust my partner utterly and to know that the primary loyalty is to me. I expect my partner to support me – in all senses of the word – and to join with me in providing a good, solid home and a stable emotional life.

When it ends: Endings are terribly difficult for me and I do everything in my power to keep a relationship going no matter how dead it has become – even to the extent of living two lives. I don't often admit this, but if things are really rocky I'll work on establishing a new relationship base before I reluctantly leave an old relationship. I intensely dislike the thought of divorce, not the least because it means dividing up the material goods. I particularly want to keep the house and the car. They're my security blanket and my status symbols. My partner will find me obstructive and obstinate in negotiating the split and I remember all the little niggles long after the divorce has gone through.

Taurus as a friend

Friendship Style: exceedingly loyal and immovable.

I'm a faithful and reliable lifelong friend as long as you remember my need for a fixed routine and no surprises. Never under any circumstances rush me and remember I hate to be left out. Given that, I am excellent company especially for artistic or edible pursuits. I want to be involved in your character's life. I excel at do-it-yourself, gardening and car maintenance. Decision making and financial planning come naturally to me. I'm pragmatic and full of good advice. But if your character is planning life changes, I'll get rattled. Some people say I'm bossy and resentful if they don't act on my advice. It's just that I can see so clearly what they need to do. If your character's crisis is to do with relationships, bear in mind that I go for the 'stay at all costs' option and do not understand emotions. And never, ever, let your character ask me to lend money. Your character should have made provision well in advance. If you want an interesting conundrum, have your character leave a wallet behind, pick a flea-pit hotel and a pizza joint and then ask me for a loan to pay off a blackmailer. Finally, whilst I am gregarious and sociable, I won't like to share your character with others, or to let go. I can be very possessive. I like what's mine to stay mine. I have been told that I'd make an excellent stalker.

Taurus as a co-worker

Co-worker Style: reliable, tenacious and utterly trustworthy.

I belong to an extremely conscientious and reliable sign – and the most hard working. Long after everyone else has packed up and gone home, I'll still be beavering away to finish what is needed for the morning – or the week after next. So, if there are vital jobs to do, people give them to dependable me. But they so often take me for granted and rarely thank me. Unless you want spectacular but slow-burning conflict, never upset me. Your character needs to remember my birthday, do whatever is promised, and never ever let me down. Your character may think a lapse is momentary but it is not. Your protagonist may forget, but I never will. One day your character will pay dear for that thoughtless remark, or moment of forgetfulness.

By the light of the old moon

Taurus moon style: embedded, jealous, conservative and immovable.

Basic drive: security.

With me for an intractable moon-sign I warn you, your character is going to have difficulty letting go. I don't move on easily. Much as I hate to admit it, jealousy is one of my most powerful emotions. I rarely forget and find it impossible to forgive. I apply the past to the present even though circumstances have changed. I've made hanging on to grievances and resentment into an art form. But I pride myself on being loyal, faithful and dependable. I've got an inherent need for security and status, but my strongest desire is for an unchanging world. People and possessions give me a sense of security. I really like my old habits. People say I'm the original immovable object and sometimes my resistance to change is so marked that I prefer to become physically ill rather than move on from a situation that no longer serves me. I've a tendency towards comfort eating as food is so useful for stuffing down my emotions. What nurtures me is getting out into nature – or into bed – and good food.

Meeting the world

Taurus rising style: materialistic, pragmatic and hard working.

When your character puts me on to go out to face the world I cover up even the most impractical of signs. My stoical mask effectively hides the most flighty nature. I may also disguise a sun-sign that is out of its depth in the physical environment. I appear to be methodical and pragmatic and totally reliable. Sometimes people say I'm plodding but they don't hesitate to load me with work. They can get a nasty surprise when the sun-sign I'm masking breaks through. I loathe change. Security is really important to me and no matter how much of a square peg in a round hole I may be, it takes dynamite to get me out of my nevertheless comfortable rut.

Taurus compatibility rating:

Aries*; Taurus*****; Gemini***; Leo***; Virgo*****; Libra**;
Scorpio*****; Sagittarius**; Capricorn*****; Aquarius***;
Pisces****

Chapter 8

Gemini
The Twins

♊ 21 May – 20 June

I wasn't kissing your daughter, sir – I was just whispering in her mouth.

Chico Marx (Aries sun, Pisces moon, Leo rising)

Crib sheet

First impression: Wired. Always on the move.

Appearance: Expressive, thin, wiry, scholarly and youthful with long slender limbs. Piercing bird-like eyes under tapering brows in a sharp, narrow, symmetrical face.

Stance: Enquiring. Head tilted to one side. Nervous, never still, constantly moves and talks with the hands.

Dress: Likes greys and blacks, spots and stripes, symmetry. Quirkily fashionable or professorial.

Favourite Word: Why?

Says: 'I think … ' 'So?' 'Yes, but … ' 'Why don't we … '

Never says: Sorry.

Career: Spin doctor, journalist, writer, computers, linguist, teacher, salesperson, distance learning, communications, public relations.

Archetype: The fixer.

Shadow: The compulsive liar.

Likes: Chat rooms, symmetry, books, films, partying, puzzles, yoga, raquet sports, writing, computers, music, shopping, anything cool.

Dislikes: Boredom, being alone, keeping silent, rules and regulations.

Money: Easy come, easy go.

Dreams: Of a multi-media, multi-cultural world.

Getting to know Gemini

Personality style: Bright, lively, inquisitive and communicative, never grows old. A natural insider.

Other people tell me that I'm multiple personalities in one package. They say I constantly change and will argue black is white one minute, black is black the next, and then white is black without even noticing. But it's just that I like to explore all the options. Apparently I'm charming one moment, acerbic the next, facile and superficial, but incredibly perceptive and intuitively aware at a very deep level. I know I'm easily bored. Mercurial and changeable, liking tricks and paradoxes, I sometimes have deep depressions. I usually treat them with a large gin. I need other people as a sounding board for my ideas and simply have to talk. I frequently have several jobs, innumerable interests, and am the original Mr Fixit – or I know someone who can. I love networking and bringing people together. People accuse me of being emotionally illiterate as I think rather than feel. I can't understand why. Agreed, I enjoy *discussing* feelings, preferably someone else's rather than my own, and have no desire to immerse myself in emotion. I really struggle when anyone, including me, is emotionally traumatised or challenged.

With my enquiring mind I'm one of the most communicative, flirtatious, inventive and persuasive signs in the zodiac. Pillow talk, phone sex, and internet chat rooms suit me. But, while delighting in the idea of love and friendship, I'm not so sure about lifelong involvement. Mind you, I need other people as a foil for my thoughts. I'll share a secret with you, as an eloquent Gemini I can convince anyone of anything, and less wily signs find themselves finessed into saying yes without really knowing how they got there. As do I.

What Makes Gemini Tick: I absolutely hate to be bored and freely admit to being mischievous and positively lethal if my mind is not happily occupied. Gazing into someone's eyes for hours on end is my idea of hell – unless I'm talking or texting at the time! And never ask me to keep a secret. I was born to gossip and somehow it just slips out. I need other people to make me spark. I delight in word games and verbal fencing, and feel alive only when sharing ideas or satisfying my insatiable curiosity about the world. I flit seamlessly from one thing to another, often without even noticing until someone points out that my viewpoint or my personality has changed. Other signs find it hard to keep up, or to understand that, for me, truth is whatever I happen to be embracing momentarily. It can – and will – quickly change, and I often play devil's advocate to keep things interesting. So, when I vow eternal love, for instance, it is neither truth nor lie. It is what it is *at that moment*. I'm not deliberately duplicitous, half the time I don't know how I really feel and so I'm fooling myself as well.

The Gemini shadow: My uncanny ability to ferret out secrets and inability to keep those secrets makes me a smooth operator, a cunning character that can never quite be relied upon. Did I mention callow? Or capricious? I'm two-faced and duplicitous and simply love spreading salacious gossip. To be absolutely honest, I'm unable to distinguish truth from fiction half the time, especially when I've spun a load of half-truths and downright lies. I get caught up in my own deceits but I can be gullible too. Tell me an interesting tale and I'm hooked. I'm a natural con-man well suited to white collar crime or impersonation – oh yes and identity theft – but I also make an excellent cat burglar, an adept disseminator of disinformation, and if you're looking for a whistle blower or covert informer, a leaker of the ultimate secret of secrets, here I am!

Gemini speak: "Of course there's no such thing as UFOs. That Roswell secret report? Nah, the US Government has denied it, said it was all a hoax. But that alien did look like the real thing and so many pilots have seen lights and cigar-shaped ships. It can't all be faked. They must know what they're looking at. Wasn't something leaked a year or two back about the huge number of UK sightings? I'm sure there's something in it. I think I'll book for that Crop Circle conference so I'll see the evidence for myself." [Conversation with a Gemini friend who, for reasons that will be obvious, doesn't want to be identified.]

Your Gemini male character

I've been thinking about a word to describe me. Charming? Winsome? Mercurial? Sparkling? Witty, satirical, sarcastic, informative, inquisitive, derogatory or defamatory? There are so many that fit. I'm a *puer* at heart. You never really know me. I'll always surprise you with a sudden *volte face*. I'll talk myself into existence – and out again – and evolve faster than you can think. You can write me as a superficial and yet incredibly complex, multi-layered character and I won't be offended at anything you say. I'm just curious to see what you make of me. I change disposition in a moment, switching before your ears. I hold one opinion, then argue the opposite, and swing back again. As a writer you need to be agile to keep up. I can be quickly overtaken by black moods when, for once, I insist on being left alone. Just when you begin to despair, my mood inexplicably lightens. Dangle a conundrum in front of me and I'll be away again.

While I have intellectual depths, I don't know how to make a lasting emotional connection or how to be intimate at that deep level where emotional sharing takes place. Instead, I dance lightly over the surface of life. I have an insatiable need for people. Wired, I bounce around a gathering mixing, fixing and getting it on. I have several mobile phones and a tablet or two because I can't stand call waiting. I simply have to talk even in my sleep. And, I cannot resist the lure of an enticing woman, or a good debate. I never grow old, my face remains unlined, my chat-up lines still work, and I am charming and mentally active to the end. I have to admit I'm elusive and prefer never to face the consequences of my actions. But somehow I lead a charmed life. The gods love my untruths and my dissemblings. They smile on my schemes and honey my words. Concepts like eternity, dependability and commitment, while intellectually diverting, have no real meaning to me. You'll never have my full attention but, amusing, intriguing, and bemusing, I will always be an engaging companion who knows how to have fun.

Your Gemini female character

I'm even more mercurial than my male counterpart. I can be slinky and seductive or, in a flash, cool and aloof. I get into toy boys not because that makes me look good, but rather because I haven't aged. I revel in youth, beauty, wit, and playfulness. I'm more interested in deep relationships than my male counterpart because I like to know what makes people tick but I really don't understand commitment and emotional intimacy – or eternal fidelity, so boring. Other people's feelings are fascinating, but I'm often told I'm totally out of touch with my own. You can count on me to enthusiastically embrace the next good idea – no matter how ill-advised or badly thought out that may prove to be. I'm like a mirror, reflecting back what's around me, picking it up and making great leaps of intuition to find a new perspective. A word of warning, don't trust me with secrets, gossip is my life blood. I'm highly observant and a great commentator on life so I will make an excellent narrator for your tale.

Gemini in love

Love style: Flirty, flighty, inconstant and superficial. Says 'I love you' but doesn't know what that means.

A quick fling is fine, but I sometimes spend more time fantasizing about sex than actually participating. Not that anyone would know that to listen to me, in my head – and, therefore, on my tongue – I always have the most wonderful sex life. I find it difficult to be restricted to only one partner and often have two on the go at once. I'll marry late, particularly as I enjoy platonic friendships with both sexes. There's a sexual frisson to those friendships that just might develop further. Mental rapport is more important than physical considerations and I want a partner to be a companion in all senses of the word. Even when I succumb to love, commitment is a problem, as is faithfulness. I rather like the separate houses or different countries style of relating. I'm sometimes so caught up in the excitement of erotic fantasies that I forget about physical relationships.

Gemini seeks: companionship, mental rapport, stimulation, freedom, mind-blowing sex, marriage is way down the list.

Seduction Technique: I use honeyed words and hearts and flowers to bewitch a prospective partner into bed. My silver-tongued subtle seduction technique promises a lasting relationship but I freely admit that this unlikely.

Flirting: I simply love to flirt, it's as natural to me as thinking –

but don't take it seriously. My clever verbal foreplay is intended to amuse rather than necessarily lead to other things.

Trust and intimacy: unknown qualities to me.

Secret sexual desire: virtual sex steps out of the monitor.

Gemini as a partner

Partnership style: versatile.

I have to say, my partner is unlikely to receive unadulterated attention, even in the first flush of love. I'm more into crowds than twosomes. There is always someone else to talk to – or flirt with. Love affairs just seem to happen to me but I'm not a philanderer, I didn't mean to end up in bed with someone else. I'm hopeless at dissembling and I know my partner is fully aware of all those surreptitious texts, the hastily erased messages, the work friends popped out for a drink with. Sociable? My partner knows all about that. Partners have told me that my greatest failing is not really listening, especially to something deeply emotional or that touches on sore points. But then, I'm not given to emotional intimacy. It is not a question of not trusting someone, I indiscriminately trust everyone, more that I don't recognise my true feelings so sharing them with a partner is impossible and I can't really empathise as I quickly get bored and look for a distraction. If my partner shares intimate secrets, he or she may be devastated to find that I've discussed them with all and sundry. I regard nothing as confidential and I'm unlikely to consider my partner's feelings in the matter.

When it ends: I'm a master of the fast exit. For me it's off with the old and on with the new. Lightly committed and with so many other things to occupy my butterfly mind, a partner's absence may not be noticed. Quickie divorce was invented for me because, by the time it comes around, I'm ensconced with my next partner. But if someone else is leaving me, be prepared for an inquest, I want to know why!

Gemini as a friend

Friendship style: garrulous, gossipy, inventive, intellectual, fickle.

Naturally gregarious, I don't go in for singularity or depth, and tend to have lots of acquaintances rather than one 'best friend'. Your character will be one of a crowd and may not always hold my attention, which can create conflict, but will have a great time, and get a new slant on life. I make a wonderful friend if your character wants a sociable, fun companion to party with or enjoys long, gossipy conversations over coffee or a bottle of wine putting the world to rights long into the night. I'm a great informer. I read all the latest books, see the in-films and take every online newspaper there is. But if your character needs a friend for deep, intimate conversations, someone who cherishes and guards secrets, look elsewhere. I might relish the chats but the secrets are all over town by morning. I was born to betray, but carelessly rather than maliciously. Unless of course your character has upset me. Then the gossip becomes vicious, I'm happy to trash an adversary's reputation anytime. Where I come into my own is when your character needs information. I'm the natural fixer, always knowing the answer, or precisely where to go. But your character had better check the facts. I'm indiscriminate in my sources. The advice is practical and to the point – unless it's about emotions in which case it's only theory. I'm happy to talk about anything and everything, the more salacious the better in fact, so this is your character's opportunity to shed inhibitions and open up. It is unlikely that I'll ever be shocked. I'm likely to come up with exciting ideas to spice up life.

Understanding Your Gemini Co-worker

Co-worker Style: bright, bubbly, breezy and chatty.

I'm at my sparkling best in an environment where communication is vital. I'm dedicated to passing on facts and figures. Most will be accurate, but it's worth checking as I can be slapdash, especially if the contents are dull, and I rarely stop to listen to instructions. I'm not above taking credit for someone else's bright idea or innovation but I contribute many of my own. I love to chat and gossip, and gossip and chat. I have all the juicy titbits and your character will hear it first from me. Unfortunately I'm prone to talking about other people behind their back – but sometimes just in earshot – but with my flair for sliding out of trouble it will look like your character was the one gossiping. I may like to trash other people but please make it clear from the outset that I'm not interested in character assassination – unless that's what your book is all about. I'll happily join in then. If your character has a go at me, I'll find an inventive way to get my own back.

By the light of the multi-faceted moon

Gemini moon style: superficial and rational.

Basic need: self-expression.

I'll whisper sweet nothings in your ear, whatever you want to hear. I want to have a meeting of minds. My intuition is strong and my greatest need is to be heard, even when I've nothing much to say. I shy away from intimacy but I'll happily discuss your emotions but stay away from feeling my own. I've had some painful experiences in the past but I don't go there. If you force me to I'll rationalise them or talk them out of existence. People say I'm given to guile and cunning manipulation of other people's feelings. I like to be socially accepted – and to be liked – and I'm not above adjusting the truth to what I think people want to hear. I often take liberties with inconvenient facts or use white lies to avoid emotional hassle. Somewhere along the line I've lost my own truth. To be honest, I sometimes get caught up in dark thoughts that I mistake for emotions and can suffer from fleeting deep depressions. I play the role of puer, the Peter Pan figure who never grows up and who, apparently, slips through life without a care. I want to remain forever young at heart, charming everyone but attached to no one. Mental stimulation and attention from others provide vicarious nurturing. I find these an excellent substitute for emotional satisfaction.

Meeting the world
The Gemini mask: chatterbox jack of all trades.

When your character puts me on to meet the world I'm instantly recognisable from the babble of words, madly texting with a phone in both hands and gesticulating wildly all at the same time. I can't speak without using my hands. I'm here to report on the world after all. Tablets were invented just for me. Networking is my forte and communication my *raison d'etre*. A Jack-of-all trades, other people say I'm a witty, silver-tongued multiple personality, too interested in everything to spend time studying one particular thing in depth. I make inspired connections and I'm always accused of flying off in too many directions at once. I admit to using a few little white lies if it keeps other people happy. I'm never really sure what I've said or what I think. It takes a pretty single-minded underlying sun-sign to keep up with versatile me.

Gemini compatibility rating

Aries***; Taurus*; Gemini*****; Cancer*; Leo***; Virgo****; Libra****; Scorpio*; Sagittarius*****; Capricorn**; Aquarius****; Pisces*

Chapter 9

Cancer
The Crab

Between her breasts is my home …
Three sides set on me space and fear, but the fourth side rests,
Warm in a city of strength, between her breasts.
D. H. Lawrence (Virgo sun, Libra moon, Scorpio rising)

Crib sheet

First impression: Sympathetic. Protective and caring.

Appearance: Placid, moon-faced, rounded body shape. As a rising sign, often plump with a generous bosom (in male or female) and pale watery eyes that peep sideways from under a fringe.

Stance: Tends to move circuitously rather than head-on. Arms are often folded over the solar plexus to protect a vulnerable area.

Dress: Cancer goes for comfortable, flowing clothes and wears a favourite outfit till it falls to pieces. Carries bags full of tut.

Favourite Word: Food.

Says: Let me look after you. What would you like, something to eat?

Never says: Anything straightforwardly. 'This is the truth, the whole truth and nothing but the truth', there's always a caveat.

Career: Cook, social worker, nursery nurse, midwife, care worker, human resources director, housing officer, hotelier, antique dealer, financial planner

Archetype: The homemaker.

Shadow: The smother-mother.

Likes: Emotional security and a secure home life, the past, food, dinner parties, anything to do with water, homemaking, flea markets, needlework, art, sailing, fishing, silversmithing, charity work.

Dislikes: The limelight. Emotional vulnerability. A partner who strays.

Money: Holds on to it, spends very cannily.

Dreams: Of the perfect home.

Getting to know Cancer

Personality style: Caring, reserved, withdrawn, cautious and well camouflaged. A natural outsider.

I'm deeply private and I need to know you very well indeed before I let you into what hides behind my tough Cancerian exterior. I'm something of a chameleon, taking on the protective colouring of what's around me and what people expect of me, hiding my true self under my shell. I'm going to reveal myself very cautiously. Other people call me complex and say I can be kind and caring or moody and secretive, strongly independent and fiercely aware of inner vulnerability. When you know me better you'll realise that despite being tough and confident on the outside, my inner world is insecure with constant emotional fluctuations. People say I'm insensitive when I shut myself off when feeling vulnerable or invaded but I have to protect myself as otherwise I feel totally overwhelmed by what I pick up. I need reassurance that I'm needed and I'm desperate to protect the people I love. But other signs say I'm a clingy smother-lover. I always seem to be misunderstood. Mind you, they are quick enough to come to me with their troubles, I've got a tender heart and I'm one of the most emotionally intuitive signs. But, be warned, I can also be ruthless and surprisingly ambitious and when my claws dig in, they don't let go easily.

What Makes Cancer Tick: Home is extremely important to me. My way of showing love is with food and if anyone passes on my food, I feel rejected. You'd better know that I'm often accused of being touchy and sensitive to the slightest rebuff. I take things very personally. Everything I do is orientated towards my security, poverty makes me feel vulnerable. I have a lot of hidden fears. But I'm ambitious too. I want to get to the top to protect my family financially. I feel poor unless I have oodles of spare change in the bank and I've always got a nest egg put by 'just in case'. Woe betide anyone who spends my money without asking. I fiercely protect what's mine and I'm not going to be taken advantage of. It might help you to know that despite a deep desire for physical closeness, I have a cyclical need to withdraw. My emotional tides are ruled by the moon and at the dark of the moon I'm at my most moody and vulnerable. Give me my space.

The Cancer shadow: Crabby? Moi? Never – and don't believe people when they tell you I'm cantankerous and moody either. Although I'm reluctant to let you under my shell as you might use what you learn against me, I can tell you that other people say that my flaw is obstinate self-reliance – and self-pity. I'm much too willing to give help to others, but I find it very difficult to ask for help even when this is desperately needed. I take offence at the slightest thing but don't show it outwardly. My tough Cancer shell hides more than vulnerability. You'll rarely know what I'm really feeling even when I'm murderous. Once my crab's claws take hold, they don't let go and there is a ruthless streak hidden deep inside my soft interior. When planning crime or misdemeanours, I reach deep into the past and money is probably involved somewhere along the line. I make an excellent forger. Should I tell you that the dear sweet old lady who stabs a victim with her knitting needle or quietly poisons the tea is probably a Cancer – male or female? Well, yes I will, because it will take the heat off me.

Cancer speak: 'It's really odd when you come back home from hospital. My only experience of any note has been to do with babies. You get the carry-tot seat holding your precious cargo back home, dump it in the middle of the floor because you are too scared to put it on the table – might fall off ?!! – then after a few minutes the sheer weight of responsibility falls with a massive 'thunk!' on your shoulders. It was a bit like that on Saturday, only it was the responsibility of getting me well that fell on my shoulders, and making sure that Stephen survived the process too. I think it is easy for the caregivers to be left out of this whole process. It has been very difficult to have all the attention directed at me so far, not only because I still don't really believe I'm ill and I hate being in the limelight, but also because I am so concerned about how Stephen is coping with it. He has been working to a magazine deadline whilst supporting me through all the initial hospital appointments, organising hospital visits, bringing me nutritious food to make up for the utter gunk I have been given, holding me when I have needed to cry – and dealing with the extreme and raw grief of knowing I have cancer. I think I have probably said quite a lot so far about feeling blessed and touched by the amount of support we are being given. What is so lovely is that Stephen has very obviously been included in those prayers too. That is so important and once again I thank you all.

It is a path we are exploring together; the days I feel well I want to be able to offer any support that he needs and that I would quite naturally have given before – and for us to have fun together. He is not to be my nurse maid. Try telling that to a Virgo!'

Margaret Cahill (Cancer sun, Virgo moon) *Under cover of Darkness; My journey through Mantle Cell Lymphoma* http://wwww.margaretcahill.wordpress.com/)

Your Cancer male character

I'm going to reveal myself to you very cautiously indeed. Understanding this complex and highly sensitive man is quite a task for any writer. At first I show you a tough, invulnerable outer shell but as you get to know me better, and particularly once you've experienced the great tides of emotion that sweep through me, you'll realise that underneath there is a vulnerable and soft-hearted man who is deeply affected by feelings. You'll perceive my neediness and the pain I feel for the suffering of others and how helpless I am at times. Particularly if I can't protect my family. But then, just when you think you've sussed me out, I'll show you my tough, not to say ruthless, side. I have a shrewd mind and am highly ambitious. I want to get to the top, and I would like your support so don't write me as a failure or a wimp – although I'll go through some interesting angst if you do. Oblique as always, I'm unlikely to ask for anything directly but I'll give you hints and sulk if you don't pick up on them.

Other people accuse me of manipulating their feelings and easily falling into an attack of the 'poor me's', or into brooding moodiness. A wise writer looks at the moon before wondering what is up. I am attuned to the luminescent orb, particularly at the new and full phases. Encourage me to take time for myself at the dark of the moon and I'll be more stable and far less moody. But if the moon is not the cause, check whether I'm sulking because of something one of your other protagonists has said. I sense a slight in what others call the most innocent of remarks, but I'm not going to tell anyone. You'll have to coax it out of me – and have that other character make a grovelling apology before I'm happy again. And as for manipulation, well there are more ways than one of getting what you want. Charm usually works for me but I'm very aware of what makes other people tick ... and I do so want to get my own way.

Your female Cancer character

I have a very strong nesting instinct and I'm prone to empty nest syndrome. People tell me I show my emotions to a greater extent than my male counterpart, but am even more prone to mood swings because of my menstrual cycle and the moon. I just know that I need my protective shell because I'm extremely vulnerable and can be sideswiped by betrayal or emotional stress at any moment. I'm a sensitive soul and cosseting and reassuring me with physical contact is more effective than asking what is wrong as I may not be able to vocalise my feelings. But! Although I am focused closely on my home and family, and at times I may put up with having my identity reflected back through a successful husband, secretly I have powerful, if well camouflaged, ambitions and may combine a career with being the perfect wife and mother. Sometimes I even sacrifice home to be a highly independent go-getter. I juggle the different facets of myself successfully, provided my home life is stable. I like to have support but I'd be interested in exploring what's revealed about myself if it isn't forthcoming. I'm not all that sure what's going on deep inside me and don't know which side of me would win so as a writer you could tell me. But bear in mind that, when emotionally challenged, my libido is the first thing to go.

Cancer in love

Love style: romantic, possessive, emotionally melding, seeking security and marriage.

For me love or friendship is an emotional melding. I want closeness and intimacy beyond words. Hiding a passionate nature under a shell of cool containment, in the safety of my home a sexy siren is revealed. Flowing with the currents of a deeply emotional nature, my passions rise and fall. Cuddles are as vital to me as sex, as is my partner's unadulterated love. Eternally romantic, once I have committed, I'm faithful and loyal, some would even say clingy and possessive. Woe betide my partner if he or she forgets an anniversary. Sentimental occasions mean a great deal to me and I expect the full works: a romantic candlelit dinner, expensive presents, and a great time in bed afterwards.

Cancer seeks: nurturing, shared feelings, protection, to be needed.

Seduction technique: Good food! Once I set my sights on someone, I approach circuitously and I seldom let go but am more likely to seduce someone I already know as that feels safer than a stranger.

Flirting: I may indulge in a little light flirting round the dinner table from under lowered eyes, but I don't enjoy overt advances, especially if already married. I keep my affairs of the heart secret.

Cancer as a partner

Relationship style: protective, cuddlesome, reassuring, possessive.

My partner is coddled, nurtured and spoiled. As soon as I've made up my mind that this is 'the one', I want to formalise the arrangement. The knot is tied, the papers signed and the house purchased. Then I set about making a home for us both. I'm extremely sentimental. I remember the day we met, when we first kissed, the first time we went to bed together as well as getting engaged, and married, and having a child, and I want to celebrate all these important occasions, preferably with the whole family present. Sometimes my partner says he or she feels they have to be overly demonstrative to satisfy my innate emotional neediness. I just want to feel secure. I express love physically to demonstrate closeness – and to act as a 'keep off' sign to other people. I do not tolerate any hint of infidelity. Even if the relationship is dying on its feet, I will do all I can to hold on and retie the knot. I tend to mother my partner and secretly I project unfinished business from childhood into the relationship in the hope that I'll find what I failed to find in my parents.

Trust and Intimacy: cautious trust and emotionally intimate if feeling safe.

What Cancer expects from partners: I don't expect, I demand loyalty and faithfulness, in a full-time, full on relationship. I'd like to be joined at the hip. There is little room for outside interests.

When it ends: My ex says this is where the real meaning of my clinging crab's claws becomes obvious. I can't let go. It puts me through emotional hell. I don't want to be uprooted. I want to stay in the house and hold onto all the possessions, especially the children. No way am I giving anything up. It's my security – unless my guilt undermines me. I'll make divorce as difficult as possible, and I may even try to seduce my partner back again. But if that doesn't work it will be an eternal grudge match.

Cancer as a friend
Friendship style: caring but possessive.

If your character needs a kind, caring, considerate and endlessly thoughtful loyal friend, look no further than me. I long for a 'best friend' to share everything with. But if your character values personal liberty, you may want to think twice – or plan some interesting conflicts along the way. I'll be in and out of your character's home constantly, arriving with sustenance 'just in case'. But I'm a great friend to have if your character wants a shoulder to cry on, or needs someone with whom to watch a sloppy, sentimental movie. I love emotion and emoting, and give an excellent back rub. Get out the old photos, sigh over past lovers, tell the story of your character's life, and I'm happy to listen, so long as it's reciprocal. Indeed, it won't be long before I start telling your character how much worse off I am. Ex-friends say I have a huge capacity for self-pity, and for manipulation. They'll warn your protagonist to watch out for my crocodile tears or the story that tugs at the heartstrings. I'm said to be a past master at getting my own way. Woe betide your character if he or she doesn't call when they say they will. I'll sulk and skulk. Your character needs to check he or she hasn't inadvertently done something to upset me, it's easy to do. But often it's more a question of my hormones and moon cycles than over-sensitivity. I'll get over it with the next moon phase. If your character can cope with these moods, I'll be a friend for life whose shrewd advice can be extremely helpful.

Understanding Your Cancer Co-worker

Co-worker style: People look on me as the social worker of the zodiac. I'm the person who makes the tea, brings cake, has the 'flu remedies waiting, and gets the birthday cards signed – in between sorting out any little problems and doing the work of anyone who is off sick. I can't help it, the urge to mother is too strong. I'm nurturing and supportive – until promotion beckons. My shell hides a deeply ambitious streak that means that one day I'll be the boss. Your character won't know that the job was applied for. I'm not upfront about it. Your character might also have applied, but I'm shrewd. I sidle in and take it before anyone knows what's happening. I've a tendency to settle old scores so make sure your character appreciates all those kindnesses I do. Tomorrow could be too late. Unless, of course, that's exactly the kind of tension you are looking for in your story.

By the light of the full moon

Cancer Moon style: clingy, touchy, a compulsive nurturer and care-giver.

Basic need: security.

I'm very sentimental you know. I look back on the past with great affection – holding on grimly with my crab's claws even when it would be better to let go. A sensitive soul, I feel things very deeply too and am so easily hurt. I'm the moodiest moon but I hide my vulnerability deep under my tough shell. It protects me from allowing my powerful emotions and neediness to surface. Did I say I'm incredibly moody? I value time to make a cyclical withdrawal in tune with the phases of the moon to process emotions and dream my dreams before I emerge again to make those dreams a reality. With a strong family orientation and a powerful imagination, rather like a chameleon I can take on other people's moods unless I'm well protected. I act like a mirror, reflecting back people's emotions so they feel I'm really sympathetic. A secure home base is essential for me and I'm accompanied by treasured possessions wherever I go. Some people say I'm the original bag-lady and that I probably invented carrierbags. I cling tightly to the past. People say that mine can be a suffocating, smothering love and cutting the emotional apron strings is challenging for me. I have a dread of an empty nest. I feel emotionally vulnerable as my needs were often not met in childhood and I want to live in the past to make it better. I'm sensitive to criticism and other people accuse me of self pity and a manipulative need to control but I crave emotional sustenance and validation of my strong feelings. Instead, I nurture other people.

The Cancer mask

Cancer rising style: social worker to the world, caring for others. I meet the world sideways on. I am rarely direct, preferring to size things up before sidling up to my objective. This circuitousness can disguise a more straightforward sun sign. I empathise with other people's feelings, reflecting them back and seeking to meet their emotional needs. Under my shell I've got a soft underbelly. Other people can hurt my feelings but I often find myself becoming the social worker to the rest of the zodiac, or acting as an earth mother who fulfils everyone else's need for nurturing. But don't be fooled, I'm one tough cookie when it comes to reaching my goals. Under my camouflage I'm ambitious and uncompromising. When I do make a move, you have to be fast to catch me. I may be circuitous but I know exactly where I'm going.

Cancer compatibility rating

Aries ***; Taurus **; Gemini *; Cancer *****; Leo*; Virgo***; Libra****; Scorpio *****; Sagittarius *; Capricorn ***; Aquarius ***; Pisces *****

Chapter 10

Leo
The Lion

♌ **23 July – 22 August**

I woo thee as the lion his mate
With proud parade and fierce prestige of presence ...
And comfortable plans of husbandhood.
 Wilfred Owen (Pisces sun and moon)

Crib sheet

First impression: Regal ruler of the jungle.

Appearance: Long-maned, striking, glancing in every mirror. Eyes are bold and seductive, body tall and well shaped although often tending to largeness.

Stance: Feline, regal, majestic, surveys a room.

Dress: Expensive clothes that make an impact. Often wears gold.

Favourite Word: Adore.

Says: 'After me.' 'Do as I say.' 'Let's play'. 'Where's the best ... ?'

Never says: After you. Can I be of service?

Career: Actor, ruler, producer, rock star, sportsman, goldsmith, judge, politician, fundraiser, cardiologist, headmaster, dictator, dominatrix.

Archetype: The Queen Bee.

Shadow: Boastful megalomaniac.

Likes: Good food. Good company. Being admired. The theatre, opera and the arts. Mirrors. Acting. Shopping. Good food and wine.

Dislikes: Being alone. Being ignored or teased. Hates looking foolish.

Money: Generous.

Dreams: Of ruling the world.

Getting to know Leo

Personality style: Strong minded and larger than life, this bossy personality is impossible to ignore. A natural ruler.

I am a drama junkie and a Queen Bee, the most flamboyant character in the zodiac. I was set on earth to rule others and expect due deference. I admit I can be snobbish and autocratic and I'm very proud. But why not? I'm the best there is. When riled or ignored I may snub lesser mortals. But usually I'm sunny, playful and generous-hearted. Love, fun and playmates are what make the world go round for me. I'm fiery and passionate. I like to see and be seen and I want to show off my assets. Watch me switch on my magnets and hold court. Everything has to revolve around me. But be aware that I need to maintain a certain dignity. I have an inherent conflict. I need adulation and excitement but I also look for security and certainty and, to the surprise of many people, I enjoy a routine. I'm quite capable of making things dramatic by my actions. Lesser signs dare to mention the word bossy. But I just wither them with a look. I like to be in control.

What makes Leo tick: I'm happiest in a warm, loving, sexually active relationship, or out playing with the pack. But I need to be the leader. I don't take a back seat! I'm very proud and woe betide anyone who goes too far with teasing or poking fun. I quickly put them down with a look. No matter how hurt I may be I'll always put on a brave face and stand on my dignity. Appearance is everything with me. I need to look good because this reflects well on me. I don't often tell people this but beneath my sunny face and ebullient manner, I sometimes lack confidence but I've learned to disguise this. I hate to be seen at less than my dignified best, hence my constant checking in mirrors and shop windows. My sign is the king, or queen, of the zodiac and occupies a place that is elevated above lesser mortals and that should be duly acknowledged. Fortunately my good-natured charm ensures that most mortals do not find this offensive. Indeed, I am usually besieged by willing subjects satisfying my need to be adored.

The Leo shadow: Much as I hate to admit it, I can be a cowardly lion at times. Many people say I'm snobbish and arrogant, a megalomaniac even, but I'm just naturally superior to other people. I don't belong with the common herd. I can freeze hell over with a look if anyone upsets my dignity. Toy with me at your peril. Remember how a cat toys with a mouse. I'd hate anyone to find me inadequate. I'm told that my flaws include susceptibility to flattery and being an obsequious flatterer in order to be accepted. I'm a sucker for good living and outward appearances. I want to be on the A-list. I've been accused of exploiting other people's weaknesses and desires for my own gain. If you're writing me into a thriller, I make a perfect con-man or an excellent crime boss controlling an empire; or, for yummy mummy porn, a natural dominatrix. Everyone obeys me and woe betide them when they don't!

Leo speak: 'I came across Mariza's live performance, in Lisboa, of 'Primavera'. I listened with burgeoning joy. About halfway through I started to cry. This was Fado taken to its ultimate conclusion. You cannot better it. Mariza's voice is pitch perfect. Her rendition is astonishing. It reaches both the sadness and the joy of spring. It is the song I would like played at my funeral, when God chooses to take me. Why? Because it is a song about life and death and joy and disintegration. It is a song about loving that life and draining it to the dregs, just like I did with the Nuits St Georges Villages that will forever live in my memory. It is a song about perfection.' Mario Reading (Leo sun and moon) (http://blog.marioreading.com/blog/)

Your male Leo character

You see me instantly. I'm the flamboyant guy with the long hair, golden medallion and a big belt buckle – even if it's metaphorical. But I'll need to be very sure of you before I unburden myself. Betray my confidence at your cost, trust is important to Leo. When you first meet me I'm larger than life. Gold is my metal and I wear it with pride. I've been told I'm vain but I ignore such puerile comments. To keep me sweet, flatter me, praise me and pay me lots of attention. I need an engaging companion to indulge my passions and numerous outlets for my creativity. I have masses of friends of both sexes. They all look up to me of course. I need them to be my willing slaves. When they are, I'm a warm-hearted, considerate protagonist. If not, you'll have a standoffish egomaniac dictator to deal with. Underneath my outer assurance, however, I'm deeply unsure. All those glances in the mirror, flicking back my mane, mask a real fear that I'm not good enough. That's why image is so important to me – although I won't admit it. I've learned to be a very convincing actor. To start out, I have an almost naïve faith in people but, once let down, my pride won't allow me to risk being wrong again. You need to understand my pride before writing my character as you can use it to add motivation and tension to the story. I hate being poked fun at, loathe making mistakes, and fear being inadequate. My pride, like my will, is indomitable and intractable. I don't bend easily and I certainly don't take orders. Try a little gentle persuasion, humour works wonders for me. Appeal to my better nature and you'll soon have me eating out of your hand. If not, watch out.

Your Leo female character

Many people call me the power behind the throne but I want to be on the throne itself, looked up to and adored. I'm sexually provocative and indefatigable, and I need to be the centre of attention. I'm a predatory female who goes out and stalks what I want like a big cat and I'll play with you like a cat would a mouse, revealing a little, and then retreating until suddenly I pounce and I've got you. I'm like a lioness with my family too. I'll defend my cubs to the bitter end. You don't write me as much as allow me to play out my character in all its awe-full-ness. You'd be wise to remember that, no matter how playful I may be, I have formidable pride and great dignity. Under no circumstances do I want to look stupid, silly or undignified. So, for happy writing, flatter me, adore me and let me be the boss. But for fascinating writing, thwart me, humiliate me and give me an opportunity to show my bounteous good heart and true courage.

Leo in love

Love style: Generous, passionate and impetuous. The love life of a Leo is never dull.

Romance is an essential ingredient for my happiness. I thoroughly enjoy the whole process of dating – the flowers, the presents, the wining and dining, a box at the opera or the best hotel suite in town. In return for bestowing my affections, I expect fidelity and protestations of undying love. I need intimacy and sexual closeness but can be naively trusting, taking people at face value and being fiercely loyal until they show themselves to be something other. Then they'd better watch out. My vanity will not allow me to chase after someone who doesn't show immediate interest, nor does my pride reveal a rebuff. But don't think I'll forget, my sign has a long memory. If I'm betrayed my claws are quickly unsheathed. Lesser signs are perturbed by what happens in a big cat-fight but my sunny nature soon reasserts itself and I know how to forgive. I have a generous heart and a tendency to lionise my partner, wanting to admire and to know everything there is to know. Secrets frustrate me as I value openness and an honest heart. I love acting out my fantasies.

Leo seeks: I demand fidelity, loyalty and fun in all relationships. I see my partner as a reflection of my own worth, so my partner needs to look good at all times.

Leo seduction technique: Despite being erotic and passionate, I sometimes like to be pursued, playing cat and mouse. Sexually provocative, I turn on my magnets and wait to see who is drawn in. People usually fall at my feet. Once my prey has been caught, megawatts are focused on the object of my affections. I have a strong sex drive and no hesitation in expressing this in torrid sex but may only be playing at love.

Flirting: I could no more stop flirting than stop the blood pounding through my heart. My partner is expected to stand by placidly whilst I flirt and flatter anyone of the opposite gender with sexual innuendo. However, my flirting should never be taken seriously.

Trust and Intimacy: I am naively trusting rather than intimate, that takes time.

Secret sexual desire: humiliation and bondage.

Leo as a partner

Partnership style: I'm not into equal partnership. I need to be in charge.

In a relationship I need to be the dominant partner. Someone who is too subservient would soon become boring for your reader – and for me. My partner is very lucky to have me. It is important for my self-image that there is someone special in my life and mistakes are not easily forgiven no matter how much I may initially deceive myself. The fixed nature of my sign means that I stick with a relationship, especially marriage – although I may toy with the fantasy, or indeed even with the reality, of other partners from time to time if I think it can be got away with. But sometimes I'm a scaredy cat at heart and stick with what I know. Cultivating humility could make my relationships run more smoothly. But that might make them less interesting too.

What Leo expects from a partner: I want a partner who responds to my passionate nature and, in return, offers enduring love. I expect my partner to understand that, no matter how often I may respond to flirtatious overtures and admiration, I'm simply indulging my ego and at heart I'm loyal. To me, loyalty means not leaving – or, rather more importantly, not getting found out – rather than eternal faithfulness. When I feel safe and secure with my partner I allow them into my inner world of fantasy and eroticism. I have a strong fantasy life and look for a playmate, someone to act out and enjoy those fantasies with me. Allowing a partner to tie me up shows an enormous amount of trust, as does exposing my feelings, and I need a lover who appreciates, and never violates, that trust.

When it ends: My pride makes it almost certain that I will leave rather than be left. Indeed, I may finish a relationship just because there is a slight chance of my partner ending it – even though I want things to stay the same. But either way I hide hurt pride beneath a dignified façade – unless I resort to a sophisticated legal battle of course. I'll fight to the death to keep what I consider to be mine, and my partner has to pay dearly for a break up. I'm always the innocent party in any divorce of course.

Leo as a friend

Friendship style: gregarious but loyal.

I make a wonderful friend. Open-hearted and generous, exuberant and larger than life, I love to play but appreciate notice of an outing because I need time to dress up and look my magnificent best. There is no better companion for a shopping spree, the opera, or a party. I indulge in good food, good wine and excellent conversation. With me for a friend, be prepared for your character to play sycophant to a Queen Bee. Remember, I crave adulation and flattery. It is most important to understand: *Leo needs attention*. Your character must be prepared to make me the centre of the universe. I'm very proud and it is easy to slight me without knowing why. If I suddenly stand tall and look distant, there has been an inadvertent transgression. Did your character tease or poke fun? Laugh at a minor mishap? Comment unfavourably on my dress? Disagree with me? All are cardinal sins in my eyes. Fortunately it doesn't take long for my joie de vivre to reinstate itself and I rarely hold grudges for long. What I do demand is that your character listens, sympathises and agonises. Make sure I phone your character or the bills will be astronomical. I'll listen to your character's troubles or plans but, sooner rather than later, the spotlight switches back to me. I can be ferocious in defending those I love. But when something, or someone, more exciting intervenes I exit without a backward glance. There are spaces in my friendship. It picks up where I left it, when I'm ready. But, I'm worth waiting for. I'm a loyal, funny and kind-hearted ally. A friend without malice, someone to treasure.

Leo as a co-worker

Co-worker style: Cooperative but Leo wants to be in charge. I quickly get personal and want a warm working environment – but one dominated by me. Your character may well find I flirt and there can be a strong sexual undertone. Ignore this at your protagonist's peril as if I feel slighted, things get frosty. But, on the other hand, don't take it too seriously. If you remember my Leo pride and my need to be admired, the working relationship runs smoothly. My generous hospitality invariably includes co-workers. Of course if you want tension and conflict in your character's life, ignoring me is just the trigger you need. Other signs say I'm a dominating egomaniac. I'm into power plays in a big way and can be surprisingly manipulative, using friendship and intimacy as ploys to gain control in the working environment. Remember that, if friendly persuasion doesn't work, I can become a despotic dictator.

By the light of the grandiose moon

Leo moon style: indulgent, hedonistic and warm.
Basic need: admiration.

With my moon in generous, affectionate and warm hearted Leo I spread my benevolence over everyone with whom I come into contact. I'm charismatic, poised and creative. I naturally attract people to me and I have an innate authority. People say I'm an excellent mentor. I'm really looking for personal empowerment and being recognised as someone special. I want to be looked up to, adored and obeyed. Other people say I'm bossy and resort to emotional games to get my own way. I admit that if I'm ignored, I retreat into wounded dignity. I have a deep desire for luxury and self-indulgence. I know I need to explore power issues and express my creative energy in the most positive way possible. I'm a little afraid of exploring the destructive emotional programming and pride that drains my power. At heart, there is something innocent and child-like about the Leo moon although prejudice and bigotry were instilled in me in childhood and I struggle to overcome that. I'm naturally wilful and I want to express the playful side of myself without behaving childishly but I sometimes fall into spoilt brat. I have a strong libido. If I'm not expressing this, my back goes out. Admiration and being special to you is what nurtures me.

Meeting the world
The Leo mask: Ebullient.

When your character puts me on to meet the world they become naturally charismatic and very, very special. I enjoy holding court – or providing a mask of confidence behind which to hide. I can disguise the most timid of sun signs. People cannot help noticing me as I regally survey my surroundings, I glow with a special radiance and, as I am a born performer, my penchant for hogging the limelight often exasperates other people. I tend to talk across people and they tell me I need to listen more as I make everything about me. Be careful how you write me. I can retreat into a cold standoffishness that is far from sunny if you upset me. I'm very sensitive to criticism. And never forget that a lion is a predator with huge ambitions and extremely sharp claws.

Leo compatibility rating
Aries****; Taurus***; Gemini***; Cancer*; Leo**; Virgo**; Libra*****; Scorpio ****; Sagittarius *****; Capricorn**; Aquarius*****; Pisces**

Chapter 11

Virgo
The Corn Maiden

♍ **23 August – 22 September**

All love at first, like generous wine,
Ferments and frets until 'tis fine.
Samuel Butler (Aquarius sun)

Crib sheet

First impression: Self-contained and efficient.

Appearance: Neat and tidy. Virgo is always well groomed. The body is usually slender and well-proportioned, the face open and helpful.

Stance: Quietly confident and grounded.

Dress: Virgo often wears a uniform. Otherwise, stylish but restrained clothes in coordinated colours that do not date.

Favourite Word: Service.

Says: Can I assist you? Let's get this right. Was that good enough? Let's tidy up.

Never says: Don't worry. Leave it until another day.

Career: Health professional, cleaner, craftsperson, scientist, inspector, analyst, critic, librarian, data processor, market researcher, gardener.

Archetype: The server.

Shadow: The neat-freak.

Likes: Order, nature, cleanliness, making lists, craftwork, team games, yoga, evening classes, charity work, chess, computers, health club.

Dislikes: Dirt, mess and superficiality. Tardiness. Hates making mistakes.

Money: Can be tight fisted, always thrifty.

Dreams: Of perfection.

Getting to know Virgo

Personality style: Quiet, restrained, patient, and extremely attentive to detail with high ideals. A natural supporter.

I like to serve others. I'm a health conscious neat-freak and can be a real 'worry guts' as mental or emotional stress goes straight to my belly. People say I'm a perfectionist given to criticism and over-analysis but I just want to get it right – and to analyse things until I get to the bottom of what's going on. I leave no stone unturned to find an explanation. I can be very cynical in the face of the unexplainable. I admit to being a workaholic. I want to keep things neatly tied up – and fret dreadfully if they are not. I can't say no so I tend to get put upon. Other people say I'm brilliant at bringing order out of chaos and I make an excellent personal assistant or carer. My high ideals and standards seem impossible to achieve and I sometimes become paralysed because of fear of failure. I'm aware of every little flaw. I've got a really powerful inner voice that criticises me and other people for failing to meet my high expectations and my sense of natural justice pervades my life. All I want is for things to be perfect. I spend a lot of my life tidying.

What Makes Virgo Tick: First appearances are deceptive with me. I may seem to be communicating freely and openly but perceptive writers may notice that, as the action progresses, they learn little more that is new or deeply meaningful about me. There is an intimacy point beyond which I do not venture even with my creator. I analyse things into tiny pieces with my laser-sharp mind but seem to be cut off from deep feelings that cannot be expressed. I'm fastidious and I'd really like to be chaste (yes, I do mean chaste but being chased would be ok with me too). But I also have a strong urge towards promiscuity and puerile fantasies. I suppose I'm a voyeur at heart. I like to talk about sex, and enjoy looking at bodies and being touched, but the messy business of the sex act itself can be a turn off. I try not to get carried away by passion or by sentiment. One of the trickiest things for the writer of my character to handle is my sign's tendency to nit-pick – and the insistence on doing everything to an exceptionally high standard. I can drive a writer to distraction if you are not careful. You have to examine every detail, dot each i and cross every t. No loose ends, no stone unturned. If I feel that something could have been done better, or that more work could have gone into it, I won't hesitate to tell you so. As a result you can feel criticised even when it was not meant.

The Virgo shadow: Taken too far, my sign's obsession with health and cleanliness can lead to a hypochondriac who always has a psychosomatic illness of one kind or another or a body image problem. And my sign's obsession with perfection and a tendency to over-analyse (sometimes I just can't stop myself) can lead to a pedantic, nit-picking, highly-critical dissatisfaction with life, or complete paralysis as I'll be afraid to begin a project for fear of failing. An unfortunate obsequiousness and a tendency to servility can lead to servitude for a Virgo. I'm 'ever so 'umble' you know. It is also said that I have a sarcastic tongue that homes in on my adversaries' weakness. My sign's ability to stand back and uninhibitedly observe can lead to voyeurism or to immersion in a steamy world of underground sexual perversion – or cooking the books. If I'm going to commit a crime it will be well planned and meticulously carried out. White collar fraud is my forte.

Virgo speak: 'So we now enter a new room. What are we putting in there? Well, a lot of that hand cleaning gel that is being advertised, for a start. It is possible, nay, likely, that my white cell count will go down very low in the next few days and I will be very open to infection. According to the MacMillan nurse people are far more likely to be infected by their own germs than those of others – barring shoppers sneezing all over you of course – which includes touching your hair, face, nose, feet, the telephone, computer keyboard. All the things around your home that you use frequently. You can imagine with Stephen's Virgo Sun and my Virgo Moon, we are having a field day! ... It becomes a whole new way of living in your own home. I accidentally scrape my hair out of my eyes, wash my hands, wipe them by mistake on the towel, wash them again, use a kitchen towel ... I'm becoming Howard Hughes! ... but you can see we have to get used to this new idea of living in our own home in a way that protects me. Protection also of course includes looking at food and supplements.' Margaret Cahill (Virgo moon) *Under cover of Darkness* blog http://wwww.margaretcahill.wordpress.com/)

Your Virgo male character
All you need to know to understand my modest and refined character is that I am seeking perfection and much of my time is spent analysing my behaviour to see whether I could have done better; that or bringing order to my external world. I cannot abide dirt or untidiness. But I also have a drive to get down to the nitty gritty of matters, to grind the corn exceedingly small. My inner critic usually allocates a low mark so you could boost

my ego by offering praise – although it makes for more interesting reading if you don't. I live with this nagging and insistent inner critic constantly, it never lets up. If I could learn to put it on one side and loosen up, I'd be a much happier man. But it is a huge task for me. My natural inclination is to look at all the fine detail, to take things to pieces, extract the essence, and then see how it measures up. The goals I set myself are impossibly high, as are the standards I try to meet. The problem is, I apply those same standards to everyone else and they have to measure up too. I'm so often disappointed. Aside from my desire for perfection, I also have to contend with my earthy, lusty nature. My inner drive, which I try to keep under control, is sensuous and sexy, but again the critic comes in, this time wearing his inner prude hat, and I can retreat into a psychosomatic ailment in response. If you could make a game out of my inner critic, consigning him to the wardrobe for the duration I'd be a much more inventive and enthusiastic lover of life. I'll let you into a secret, I rather like playing practical jokes on people and they usually have a twist in the tale.

Understanding your Virgo female character

I want to be presented as discerning and perfect, no flaws or failures for me. Although I'm highly cerebral, I'm more comfortable with my sexuality than a Virgo man. I've got the same high ideals, and that nagging inner critic and prurient prude, but somehow I can silence the urge for perfection and live in the moment, throwing my inhibitions to the winds as I promiscuously explore my innate sensuality. I have a deep desire to be helpful, though, and to be needed. Some of what I do for others boosts my own sense of self-worth. But on the whole I perform these services quietly because that is part of my nature and appreciation is a bonus I cherish but can live without.

Virgo in love

Love style: conflicted, faithful and loyal.

I'm earthy and sensual but at the same time finicky, prudish and ambivalent about expressing sexuality. I can appear quite prim on the surface but underneath have strong carnal desires that lead to some frustrating internal tensions. I'm a courteous and considerate partner but I give few displays of affection, especially in public as I reserve passion for the bedroom. My sexual style is one of cool ardour rather than ardent passion and I show love by doing things for my partner. With unquenchable curiosity as to all things sexual, until I find a life partner, I am content to play the field. Other people call me picky and pernickety. But I say I'm discriminating. I know exactly what is, or is not, a turn on for me. I'm into the rituals of courtship and romance. It takes me quite a while to commit but once the choice is made, I tend to be faithful, although in time my relationship may drift into platonic friendship as I value mental rapport rather more than sexual compatibility.

Virgo seeks: With a strong need for intellectual companionship, I want a partner who is on my wavelength and who has the same standards and ideals. I find it difficult to live with anyone who is dirty or untidy in their personal habits.

Seduction Technique: I seduce with words, spinning a mesmerising web of possibilities. My unruffled surface shows little of the earthy sensual passion of which I am capable as that is reserved for private, intimate moments. As with everything, my search for perfection leads to a cautious approach.

Flirting: I'm the quietly sexy sign of the zodiac and discreet flirtation is one of my hobbies. Witty and well-informed, I have refined verbal foreplay into an art.

Trust and Intimacy: I show cautious trust, superficial intimacy.

Secret sexual desire: starring in a porn movie.

Virgo as a partner

Partnership style: loyal, exacting and discerning.

I set exacting standards for lovers, who have to be aesthetically pleasing as well as demonstrating sexual and intellectual prowess. I expect a partner to be faithful, although the occasional fling may be forgiven. My exes say I'm exceedingly critical and nit-picking when partners don't measure up. What I look for is loyalty, intellectual stimulation and exciting nights. My intimate gatherings are carefully planned to show off my partner – and I will even clear up afterwards. Perhaps I could remind you that partners would do well to acknowledge and appreciate everything that is done for them by this willing slave. I need to be in charge of my body but at the same time I want to express my earthy sexuality with a trusted partner on the same mental wavelength who can stoke the fires of carefully managed lust into a conflagration.

What Virgo expects from a partnership: I value true partnership and shared ideals and look for support in all my endeavours. What I really seek is perfection, discernment and fidelity. I may tolerate the occasional discreet fling but hesitate to leave the long-term security of the primary relationship as home and family mean a great deal to me.

When it ends: I'm rather civilised about endings. Things do not happen suddenly, I slowly realise that a partner has become a platonic friend, and eventually one or other of us finds a new partner. Separation is easier for me than divorce, as this would be acknowledging a mistake. But when it is finally over, I need things to be tidy and ensure that all legal matters are taken care of fairly. Even after separation, I may holiday with my ex for the sake of the children.

Virgo as a friend

Friendship style: cool, chatty and reliable.

I prefer small intimate gatherings to large crowds, but I'm an excellent companion for music or theatre trips, the gym, walks in the country or a visit to a health farm. I'm full of practical advice, and very handy to have around if redecoration or repairs are needed. I'm pretty solid in an emotional crisis too, although it is analysed meticulously. Your protagonist can trust me, even share secrets as long as a promise is extracted that they remain a secret. My sign is ruled by Mercury after all, and he is a chatty kind of chap. If things go wrong, it's because your character doesn't meet my standards. I intensely dislike tardiness in any form. I'm happy to discuss the situation – if your character can take that level of criticism – and I might even laugh when the inventory of faults comes to an end and the absurdity is seen. Fortunately, I have an excellent sense of humour and the ability to laugh at myself as well as at others. If your character wants to be entertained with intelligence, he or she should phone a Virgo friend.

Virgo as a co-worker

Co-worker style: efficient, hardworking and cooperative.

Enjoying mutual projects and naturally cooperative, I make a great co-worker. I'm detail orientated and focus on what is relevant at that moment, so I'm adept at getting to the crux of the matter. I'm a natural problem solver who is able to create the highest quality with minimum resources. My motto is that if a job's worth doing, it's worth doing to perfection so I quickly become indispensable. I'm the person your protagonist goes to when in need of facts and figures, the detail is immaculate and the data reliably sourced. However, have your character remember that a Virgo co-worker is a workaholic and I can drive myself too hard. I always feel that there is something more to do and, unless swept out of work for a drink, I burn the midnight oil with resulting stress. Much as I hate to admit it, I'm something of a hypochondriac and have every remedy going for whatever ails, or is likely to ail, your character. Although my desk may seem like the best place to leave the filing or much needed research, remember that even the most willing worker sometimes has enough. Have your character say thank you – or not depending on how you want the action to go.

By the light of an immaculate moon

Virgo moon style: altruistic and meticulous.

Basic need: to be useful.

Although I'm usually more modest, let me say from the outset that I have enormous integrity, good sense, an excellent memory and razor sharp perception. I have a strong urge to organise – and tidy – and to be of service but I've also got a tendency to fall into the servitude trap. I often sacrifice myself for the needs of others. If I'm unable to follow my deep desire to be of dispassionate service, without looking for external reward or recognition, I feel subtly dissatisfied with life – as I do when I am of service out of a desire to be liked or thought worthy. Somehow that never works for me. I feel deeply disappointed when others do not appreciate my services and I often feel put upon. I really need to write my own script in accordance with my truth. I'm searching for a meaningful existence but tend to over-commit to work instead. If I could stop criticising myself, and other people, I think I could get over my belief that I'm not quite good enough. My repressed emotions often show themselves as psychosomatic illnesses and I may well be regarded as a hypochondriac by the rest of the world.

Meeting the world

The Virgo mask: Efficiency.

When your character puts me on to go out and meet the world I'm compelled to tidy it up. I mean, how much disorganisation can one sign be expected to put up with? The face I present is hard working, dependable and service-orientated. I do so want to be of service you know. I need to be useful – and appreciated for it. I appear to be cool in a crisis, analytical and detached with the flexibility to embrace change and the organisational skills to remain in control. I often lack confidence in my abilities and allow others to coerce me into support roles, or servitude. However, my mask of service may disguise a more ambitious or outgoing sun-sign which leads to an internal struggle for me. This mask gives me a dedication to a task, but it may conceal my true talents – for a time. My creativity may be blocked by more pragmatic calls on my time. Other people often ask too much of me as I organise the world.

Virgo compatibility rating

Aries*; Taurus *****; Gemini*; Cancer****; Leo*; Virgo*****; Libra *; Scorpio ***; Sagittarius ***; Capricorn *****; Aquarius***; Pisces *****

Chapter 12

Libra
The Scales

♎ **23 September – 23 October**

Come live with me, and be my love, and we will some new
pleasures prove Of golden sands, and crystal books, with
silken lines, and silver hooks.
John Donne

Crib sheet

First impression: Disarming and charming.

Appearance: Harmony of face, body and personality and an ease
of movement makes Libra singularly pleasing to look at even
when not conventionally good looking. A Libra character spends
an inordinate amount of time titivating in a cloakroom.

Stance: The face is serene, the stance is poised yet appeasing with
a smiling face, the body cuddlesome and appealing.

Dress: Always colour-coordinated and harmonious, you will
never find Libra in clashing colours or poor quality clothes.

Accessories are restrained but excellent quality.

Favourite Word: We.

Says: Yes dear. Let's be fair about this. If you insist. Shall we ...

Never says: No. What right have you ... ? I want.

Career: Judge, lawyer, diplomat, marriage guidance counsellor, interior designer, graphic artist, image consultant, art dealer, welfare worker.

Archetype: The diplomat.

Shadow: Fawning people pleaser.

Likes: Mirrors, people, social occasions, peace at all cost, dating, pair-sports, dancing, health club, interior design, craft, shopping, cinema, nightclubs.

Dislikes: Disagreements, unfairness, being hurried or asked to decide.

Money: Very shrewd and careful with cash.

Dreams: Of the perfect marriage.

Getting to know Libra

Personality style: I'm the ultimate people pleaser, sociable, charming. A natural joiner.

I'm such a charming, laid-back character that I find it virtually impossible to say no. I seek fairness and harmony, and rarely show anger as I desperately want to please people. I adapt, adjust and compromise to keep the peace – until one day my personal needs break through with great force. Everyone is shocked then, especially me. I'm renowned for being diplomatic and tactful but sometimes I'm highly critical and judgemental. They say my sign is indecisive, but this is not strictly true. Yes, I find decisions difficult and choices confusing, but this is because I see everything from several different perspectives and need time to weigh up the pros and cons. It's much easier to go along with everyone else. Under all my sugary sweetness there can be a lethal nastiness. What often surprises people is how ambitious and go-getting I am. Yes I would prefer to flatter, wheedle and manipulate, getting my own way through sheer *niceness* but I am one tough cookie underneath. At heart I'm really out to look after me.

What makes Libra tick: relationships make me feel complete. I'm a natural people pleaser, conflict makes me uncomfortable, and everything I do is orientated towards creating a harmonious world. My desire for peace at all costs may mean that I compromise to a point where I lose sight of myself and my personal values. This offers you an interesting point at which to begin a story. I intuitively respond to people's needs, putting my own on hold until they erupt without warning. The rest of the world reels from the results. I'm searching for perfection, everything has to be *right* and *fair*. I want to look good, need a pleasing ambience, make sound judgements, and dream of a perfect relationship. But I have a tendency to judge people harshly on appearance rather than inner qualities. The assertive side of my nature emerges when one compromise too many is called for. There are standards below which I do not go. People who view me as a push-over are surprised when I suddenly dig in and become immoveable. This is the moment when they understand that my extremely pleasant façade disguises an equally tough interior.

The Libra Shadow: My courteous face hides a sharp tongue and wheedling insincerity. I'm often accused of being utterly selfish, manipulative and lazy. I want to be comfortable and so I overlook inadequacies and gloss over problems to keep the peace. Promises are facilely made and many disappointments follow. Then I find a way to blame others for failures. People tell me I can be extremely critical and judgemental. I know that I am suspicious and mistrustful – when I'm not naively trusting the whole world. I am a person of extremes. They accuse me of resorting to lying and cheating to get my own way. For that reason I make an excellent conman or spy, especially of the *femme fatale* variety. Mine can be a toxic niceness and a serial killer or skilled manipulator lurks behind my charming façade.

Libra speak: 'By this time, Bill and Maud had arrived at the local Batch and accepted [the invitation] joyously. "Now don't propose to me again," I told Bill. "You've done it three times already in Vila, and I'd like someone else to have a go."' Angela Sewell *Dear Gloria: Living in the Pandemonium.*

Your Libra male character

Suave, charming, impeccably groomed, promiscuous and eminently fanciable, I'll wind you round my little finger whilst professing that your happiness is all I care about. Charm is one of the ploys I use to ensure I get what I want in life with the least hassle but I want to be presented in the best possible light. Not that you'll mind, I'm such pleasant company and so romantic that you'll willingly fall into my trap. I'm the winsome man who adjusts to everyone's needs, and who romances the world relentlessly. Until, that is, it inconveniences me. Under my nice façade, there is a selfish, lazy streak and a stubborn one. I cannot be coerced. I make promises, but won't keep them, and I am a master of those little white lies that avoid me having to hurt people's feelings or inconvenience myself. The reality is that I prefer to be economical with the truth rather than face an argument. I won't put myself out. The ambiance of my environment is important. I need pleasing surroundings, I'm made physically uncomfortable by mess, and clashing colours give me a migraine. For an interesting story stick me somewhere conflicted or downright grotty. A surprisingly tough and mean streak will emerge.

Your Libra female character

I am alluring and eminently beddable. I long to please you unless it puts me out in any way. I can't be doing with that for long. I flatter every man I meet, making him feel like the only one for me but I don't mean it. Frequently late for appointments, I apologise profusely and charm everyone. I am a woman with an enormous sense of style. My appearance matters to me and I would prefer you not to disarray my carefully arranged hair, or rumple my immaculate clothing even in the most passionate clinch. Be gentle around me or you may meet the steely, hidden side of Libra that wants things all my own way. I am tough and uncompromising – once I make up my mind. If you want your story to run smoothly don't confuse me with choices or conflicts. Flatter me, take me on shopping trips, create a harmonious atmosphere and never complain when I am late. On the other hand, if you want an interesting plot put me out of my comfort zone and watch the pushy, assertive, ambitious side of my nature manipulate my way out. I'll have no problem sleeping my way to the top if that's what it takes. I have a passion for perfection and, although, I make many compromises to achieve personal harmony, in the end I want things to be *right*.

Libra in love

Love style: I feel incomplete without a partner but can be flirtatious and promiscuous.

I have been blessed with sexual charisma and gentle charm. In love with love, I'm naturally flirtatious and have an innate ability to relate to everyone, making each one feel the centre of my world. Relationships make me complete and I prefer being one half of a couple to independent solitude. I yearn for a soulmate and the whole business of romance is essential to me. I'll appease and please, adapting to my partner so that my relationships are always harmonious. Indeed, I often lose sight of myself. Then suddenly, I have to be me again. At that point, my partner may discover that I am not quite so nice after all.

What Libra Seeks: I desire elegant sex, romance, my other half, a lasting union, more romance, marriage and fidelity.

Seduction technique: Slinky and seductive, I'm laid back but determined. I prefer allurement, flattery and guile to blatant pursuit but I always get my wicked way through sheer charm, or bewitchment if necessary. By focusing all my attention on a prospective partner I lure the object of my desire into my arms.

Flirting: I can no more stop flirting than stop pleasing you. I practise my wiles on everyone but concentrate more on the opposite sex. It rarely means anything, it's just a habit, but I can be surprisingly tough in my pursuit of the ideal partner.

Trust and intimacy: I am totally trusting, intimacy personified – on the surface.

Secret sexual desire: darkly erotic, forbidden pleasure or domination.

Libra as a partner

Partnership style: Relationships are extremely important to me and so I work at them, taking care not to conflict with my partner.

I put my sexual needs or my desires on hold, or switch them on, to please or accommodate my lover. I'm sociable and I like to have people around but usually remain loyal to one partner. I'm perfectly capable of having a discreet affair to take care of my carnal urges though. I enjoy snuggling up with a partner but can focus my attention on someone else. Although I may appear to be totally absorbed in that person, my partner is expected to know that I'm not being disloyal. I'm simply enjoying the social interaction. When it's time to leave, I return to my partner and do not understand a sulky or angry reaction – which can make for useful tension in a story. If that happens I do everything possible to smooth things over. I put my partner first in everything, adapting and adjusting to every whim. As a result, people tell me I lack congruency and authenticity, as though the person I am has become lost in what someone else wants me to be. At some point in my life, I need to rediscover who I really am when I'm no longer 'half of ... '

What Libra expects from a partner: Although marriage is not vitally important to me, commitment is. I want to be seen to be in a solid partnership. The security of a lifelong bond makes me feel comfortable with life. However, whilst I want fidelity and faithfulness, my ability to compromise means that I may accept a partner's tendency to stray, or even subconsciously expect it. My natural instinct is to make allowances, to apologise for the lack of whatever is missing from the relationship. This is particularly so where my desire for relationship at any cost has won out over my desire for perfection. I hate admitting to a mistake but, somehow, I inwardly blame myself for everything that goes wrong rather than ending an unsatisfactory liaison.

When a relationship ends: Hating confrontation, I want to be terribly fair and find it hard to apportion blame properly, and invariably apologise to everyone concerned. There are no arguments, things are divided up equally, and matters are tended to with a minimum of fuss. But there is firmness and a point beyond which I will not go. I'm not a soft option as my partner will discover if the split isn't just and equable.

Libra as a friend

Relationship style I'm thoughtful and caring.

If your character is attuned to the same things, I'm a friend for life. I'm a sociable, cultured soul who enjoys the arts and aesthetics, good food and excellent company. We can party or have intimate dinners to discuss our deepest feelings. I'm into sharing emotions in a big way. I may enter into a polite debate, but I'm unlikely to fight over anything, preferring to end the friendship rather than disagree. I keep the peace no matter what and can calm even the most argumentative of people. However, you need to know that this does not make me the most truthful person in your character's life. Little white lies are common and I'm unrepentant when caught out. I tell your character what he or she wants to hear, or what I thought your character wants to hear. Anything that might cause pain is skirted around. If it's plain, unvarnished truth your character is seeking, look elsewhere. If it's advice, I'm shrewd and extremely helpful. Your character is shown all sides of the picture, and given all the options. Just don't expect me to make the decision. I'm a terrible timekeeper. How your character deals with this will depend on their own sun-sign. I'd rather you didn't make them impatient with me.

Libra as a co-worker

Co-worker style: I'm extremely cooperative and go all out for a harmonious working environment.

I delight in my skill as a team builder and love to be a co-worker. I ensure harmony reigns in the workplace, and put all those finishing touches that make it a comfortable place to be. My diplomatic skills smooth over ruffled feelings or points of disagreement and life flows wonderfully smoothly. Until you ask me to make a decision. If you're wise, you'll keep me out of the decision-making loop by presenting the finished product and asking how it can be improved on. Don't offer this or that choice – unless of course you want to create conflict. In which case, let yourself go. I'm also incredibly ambitious behind my charming façade, which means more than a little covert back-stabbing along the way.

By the light of the sugary moon

Libra moon quality: pleasing but inauthentic.

Basic need: harmony.

I offer cooperation, diplomacy and creative compromise. An ability to get on with everyone, and a desire for a tranquil life although, where possible, I'll fight to right injustice. I need to be needed – and to be liked. I only feel whole when I'm in a relationship so I adapt, adjust and compromise whenever I'm faced with other people's requirements. I'm a natural-born people pleaser but secretly, I want to be in control. I want to have my unacknowledged needs met – not that I'm going to ask but I'll wheedle and hint and maybe someone will notice. Unless my surroundings are harmonious, I'm desperately uneasy. Faced with a room of uncongenial people, clashing colours and environmental discomfort, I feel physically ill. Although I'm a born romantic, a secure relationship is more important than true love, and I must always please my partner. I've fallen into the pattern of doing what is 'nice' rather than what is right, what I've been taught is 'pleasant and acceptable'. I can be sugary sweet and terribly inauthentic. One of my greatest fears is of facing emotional pain: mine or someone else's. I believe I could easily die if I have to undergo such pain. Living according to my own aspirations and paying attention to my own needs would nurture me.

Meeting the World

The Libra mask: Placating and nice.

When your character puts diplomatic me on I charm the world, sliding this way and that in a desire to please and be liked. People notice me because I'm always well dressed but I sometimes swing between two extremes. I get on with everyone and relationships are extremely important to me but this may be the mask behind which a darker sun-sign hides. My equable, people-pleaser temperament conceals an ambitious, and somewhat ruthless, heart which can be extremely selfish but I get my way by misdirection rather than confrontation and demands depending on the sun-sign I am covering. However, I have a strong sense of fairness and will fight to the death for the under-privileged and the mistreated as I long to right rights and see justice done.

Libra compatibility rating

Aries*****; Taurus***; Gemini***; Leo*****; Virgo**; Libra*****; Scorpio**; Sagittarius*****; Capricorn***; Aquarius***; Pisces***

Chapter 13

Scorpio
The Scorpion

♏ 24 October – 21 November

No thorns go deep as a rose's
And love is more cruel than lust.
Algernon Swinburne (Aries sun and moon, Pisces rising)

Crib sheet

First impression: Intense and unfathomable.

Appearance: Magnetic, hypnotic. charismatic. Eyes are dark and brooding, the gaze pierces the soul. Hooked, hawk-like nose and strong eyebrows.

Stance: Stands like a bird of prey or skulks like a spider waiting to pounce. Brooding, still and menacing, or watchful and 'come-hither'.

Dress: Wears dramatic clothes, likes leather, and invented power dressing.

Says: Very little but sees everything.

Favourite Word: Secret.

Never says: Anything that reveals the whole truth.

Career: Detective, doctor, hospice worker, psychiatrist, gynaecologist, nuclear weapons designer, sewage worker, butcher, spy, power-broker, forensic scientist.

Archetype: The raptor.

Shadow: Venomous.

Likes: Power, mysteries, sex, the erotic and the exotic, dangerous sports, planning revenge, metaphysics, martial arts, jogging, motor racing, bar-hopping or clubbing, self-improvement, computers.

Dislikes: Openness, exposure. Positively hates change.

Money: Very shrewd, money equals control.

Dreams: Of controlling the world.

Getting to know Scorpio

Personality style: I'm difficult to get to know, power hungry and manipulative, charismatic and charming. A lone outsider.

I'm deeply mistrustful so I prefer to keep my secrets closely defended but I penetrate those of other people with glee. I'll write my own character, warts and all. I'm extremely perceptive and alert to nuances, drawn to unravelling mystery and uncovering secrets. I'm compulsive and obsessive, not afraid to go where others fear to tread. I explore all the taboo areas of life and there is a strong self-destructive streak to me, I have to challenge death head-on. I've got a sarcastic tongue, so watch out. I'm deliberately enigmatic and I dwell on the past, hoarding my vengeful thoughts. However, I've got enormous resilience and tenacity, I never give up. It doesn't take much to offend me. Anyone who has anything to do with me needs to be warned about the Scorpio sting in the tail. I can't help it. I lash out without warning and without provocation. It's my nature so don't take it too personally.

What makes Scorpio tick: I keep my secrets hidden in dark corners, which makes my sign one of the most intriguing of the zodiac to write. But you have to have the same degree of perspicacity as me to penetrate my depths. Mystery and mesmerism are part of my magnetic charisma. My public face gives absolutely nothing away. Beneath, I'm compulsively secretive, pathologically cautious, paranoid, strictly controlling and emotionally defensive, and that's only for starters. Getting to know my character is an enormous challenge but I have an immensely sexy and intriguing persona that makes me almost irresistible. Gentle and tender signs would do well to steer clear though! My inner self is often a lot less confident than the outer façade suggests which is why I protect myself so well. Paradoxically I need other people and, as a result, feel emotionally vulnerable, especially when in the grip of the obsessional emotional tides that sweep through my inner being – not that anyone would know from my external appearance. I keep things strictly under wraps. Control and power is important to me, of my emotions and the environment.

The Scorpio Shadow: My obstinate shadow is venomous and spiteful, addictive and hugely self-destructive – and deeply possessive of people and possessions even when I have no need for them. If it was once mine, it's always mine. I am a touchy, brooding, paranoid soul that seeks total control over others, but for such a power-hungry sign, I can be surprisingly masochistic. Prying or upsetting me results in a vicious tongue lashing. I'll give no warning as you approach dodgy ground. The first you know about it is when my sting lands or my tongue bites. If you're looking for a protagonist that specialises in treachery and perfidiousness, I'm the one. I meet a lot of death in my life. Murder, mystery, deceit, addictions and the occult all are grist for the writer of my Scorpionic character. I'm especially suited to leading a double life. The spy or the detective is my forte but don't expect me to reveal which side I'm really on.

Scorpio speak: 'I've had a mistress for the last year. I know I told you I didn't when you questioned me over all those phone calls, but I've just been away with her for a week. If you were stupid enough to believe me when I denied it that's your problem. I'll stay tonight and then leave tomorrow. That maintenance agreement I promised to sign in case we did split up after our twenty years together? No, I don't think so. I have no obligation to you even if you did put all your money into my company when I first started up. Pay it back? No chance. You're on your own now sweetheart. No one will want you at your age.' [Scorpio ex-partner]

Your Scorpio male character

Deeply secretive, I won't reveal myself voluntarily, and you need to tread warily in seeking insights. Don't make me feel you are invading my privacy. Even when you think you've got the measure of me, I'll always surprise you. Once I know that you understand me, however, I am relieved. I, of course, have already sussed out everything about you. I can see into your very soul. I know all your weak spots. Unless you relish being seduced and laid bare do not contemplate a writing relationship with a Scorpio man. I pride myself on being inscrutable and one of the most complex and darkly emotional characters in the zodiac. I hide, I skulk, and then I sting without warning. But, I can be charming, charismatic, magnetic and very, very sexy. It all depends on my mood. One moment I'm brooding and insensitive to anyone's feelings but my own, the next I'm a seemingly charming and considerate character who subtly manipulates others to where I want to go. I simply cannot live on the surface of life. I take you into the depths. I have an urge to go where angels fear to tread and to explore all that is taboo and hidden. My carnal urges are powerful but my control is tight.

One of my strongest lessons in life is to master the enormous power that smoulders inside me without destroying myself or others in the process. My Scorpio world can be one of paranoid fears, compulsions and powerful addiction. Secretly, I am deeply insecure and conflicted. If you accept this, you can help me come to terms with the blackest part of myself. I'm enormously courageous and shining a light into the darkness brings to light the plutonian richness of my enigmatic sign.

Your Scorpio female character

I'm torrid and tantalizing sharing the same intensity, the same magnetism and the same compulsive need for secrecy and power as a Scorpio man. I too sting without warning, especially when I perceive there is danger, and my insecurity takes me into some dark emotional spaces. But I am fiercely loyal, seductive and highly erotic. I like to dominate. Being helpless creates an enticing tension within me though. Sometimes I go there willingly just to experience what it's like. All dark places draw me in. If you allow me the private interior space I need, and recognise that intimacy is hard for me, I slowly learn to trust you. Once you have gained my trust, I'll introduce you to the dark fantasies and fears of my interior world, and the obsessions and compulsions that rule my life. Embrace them, and I'm yours for ever.

Scorpio in love

Love style: I'm passionate, intense, possessive, and very, very jealous.

I belong to one of the most sexually intense signs and my stamina is legendary, as is my talent for seduction. My libido runs deep and strong although little shows on the surface. 'Still waters run deep' perfectly describes my sexual style. Sex is more appealing than love. Intensely private and protective of my own feelings, a fear of being controlled holds me back from surrendering fully to the dance of love although some of my sexual encounters are tantric in their intensity. Enigmatic and unfathomable, I say more with silence than other signs do with words. Compulsive in my search for sexual gratification, I can be manipulative or forceful in pursuit. I rarely confuse lust with love and my red hot passion burns as brightly for a passing fling as it does for the love of a lifetime. While I am loyal, I may not be faithful. The two things are entirely different. I lead a double life. I revel in swift flings and torrid but unemotional sex but compulsively return to old lovers. If I'm not getting enough sexual excitement and my desire for intrigue is not being satisfied I fantasize, turn to porn, and cannot understand why a partner would object to psychological unfaithfulness. However, I'm one of the most jealous and possessive of the zodiac signs so my partner is not allowed the same freedom.

Scorpio seeks: erotic sex, power, marriage, commitment, loyalty.

Seduction technique: I deliberately use my personal magnetism to make my sexual pull irresistible. Amorous intensity smoulders beneath my surface, its force being *felt* rather than seen. My pheromones draw people in. When I seduce I size up the carnal potential, move in slowly, and await results. Once aroused, however, I'm fully capable of forcing sex upon someone, but it may well be a fleeting lust.

Flirting: I flirt with slyly intense glances and intimations of a mystery to be revealed. I can hypnotise most other signs into bed before they've noticed.

Trust and intimacy: I'm deeply suspicious and have little time for intimacy.

Secret sexual desire: I will never reveal this but how about a little auto-eroticism for starters?

Scorpio as a partner

Partnership style: I am a seductive lover who knows exactly how to turn a partner on but who keeps my personal desires strictly under wraps.

Once I finally succumb to love rather than lust, I'm a loyal partner but I expect my lover to act out some of my darker sexual urges. In a committed relationship, my intensely emotional and erotic self is slowly revealed. With my obsessive nature, I spend a great deal of time fantasizing about my beloved and keep a jealous watch on my partner's activities. My partners say I can be emotionally insensitive. It would be helpful if I could open up, but it is against my nature to do so and partners need to tread gently. They also need to be aware that they are not immune from my sting. While I value a partner who understands my moods, I nevertheless shy away from one who knows too many of the secrets of my heart.

What Scorpio expects from a partner: I can be intense about partnership and demand loyalty and enthusiastic participation in my deepest, darkest urges. Much as I'd like to be emotionally self sufficient, I have a need for other people and at times an almost mystical connection is created with my partner. That does not mean, however, that I will share myself fully. Something is always held back and perceptive partners are aware of this. I want a partner who does not intrude.

When a relationship ends: I'm highly resistant to change and do not like endings. Even if it is me who is leaving, love quickly turns to spite and I deliberately make things as difficult as possible especially with my barbed tongue and practised lies. I want to hold on to my assets at all costs and I bear a grudge for a very long time.

Scorpio as a friend

Friendship style: I'm intense, secretive and loyal. I have powerful insights into all matters hidden and forbidden. You may well find that, when the friendship has matured, your character is honoured with confessions of my previously untold secrets. I have journeyed into the underworld and your character may find the secrets shocking but never reveal this or the trust will not be regained. If your character can provide reassurance that my feelings are perfectly natural, it will relieve some of my deep guilt and help me lighten up – but internal dilemmas may be generated between loyalty to a friend and a need to pass the information on for the good of others. What do you do when a friend confesses to murder or abuse? But be warned, never, ever, reveal Scorpionic secrets or suffer the consequences. When it comes to telling me your protagonist's secrets, you won't have to! Everything is laid bare to my penetrating gaze before your character unburdens him or herself. There is little that shocks or surprises me and your character can find profound emotional support during the traumas and dramas of life, and some sage advice on how to meet challenges. I have a fun side and take partying seriously. I'm the original sex, drugs and rock'n'roll sign but I like sophisticated entertainment too, and clubbing. An ideal companion for a murder mystery weekend or any activity that requires detective work, I particularly like ferreting out secrets but may channel this into tarot readings and the like. I'm deeply interested in metaphysics.

Understanding Your Scorpio Co-worker

Co-worker style: I'm loyal and hard working, but keep off.

I'm inscrutable, and said to be something of a control freak, but I'm also conscientious and interesting to have around. I intensely dislike change so it is unwise for your character to rush in with revolutionary ideas. They need to be introduced gradually. But think what fun you as a writer can have with that! One thing your character can rely from me is loyal support – until the back stabbing kicks in or the sting in the tail lashes your character without warning or cause.

By the light of the dark moon

Scorpio moon style: intense and brooding.

Basic need: power.

Mine is an alienated, solitary moon. I crave emotional melding and control and have a deep fear of abandonment and rejection. It takes time for me to trust, although I'm capable of giving all to my partner. But if that trust is broken, it is a very long time indeed before I trust again. If my intense jealousy is triggered for whatever reason, the perpetrator had better watch out. I believe that revenge is a dish best eaten cold. I tend to prejudge the present in the light of my past pain – and there's been plenty of that. My passage through life has been traumatic and dramatic but I'm a born survivor. I have many addictions and contradictions but I also have a tremendous capacity for self-transformation. I make a fearless guide for people who are exploring the dark places with which I am so familiar. I can see way below the surface and am used to dwelling in the depths. My need is for emotional intensity and strong commitment. Anything less makes me insecure. I hold onto the past and to entrenched emotions such as resentment or jealousy so my needs tend to be compulsive and forceful, erupting from the depths. Mine is a cathartic moon that takes many trips down into the places other people fear to tread. Facing my own toxic darkness transforms my experiences into fertile compost for growth and sets me free from the tyranny of my emotions. I thrive on other people's secrets.

Meeting the world

The Scorpio mask: Secretive and inscrutable.

When your character puts on my poker face, the world had better watch out. I am the most intense rising-sign and I have strong powers of endurance. My interaction with the world is impassive and impenetrable, I give nothing away. No matter what's going on inside, my exterior is calm but my perceptive gaze lays bare other people's secrets. I often make other people squirm. I've got the power to achieve whatever I set out to do and I mask less determined and unconfident sun-signs. My magnetic personality pushes things through, or manipulates its way to the top. I don't care how I do it. I often find myself involved in power struggles and world conflicts. With my compulsion to explore all the taboo areas of life and all that is dark and hidden, I sometimes seem to be on a self-destruct mission although I've got a strong survival instinct so I usually escape harm.

Scorpio compatibility rating

Aries ****; Taurus *****; Gemini **; Cancer ****; Leo ****; Virgo**; Libra **; Scorpio ***; Sagittarius*; Capricorn ***; Aquarius ****; Pisces *****

Chapter 14

Sagittarius
The Archer

♐ **22 November – 21 December**

For lust of knowing what should not be known
We take the Golden Road to Samarkand.
James Elroy Flecker (Scorpio sun, Gemini moon)

Crib Sheet

First impression: Enquiring and tactless.

Appearance: Coltish. Long, horsy face, rangy body, athletic, good legs. The face is often ruddy or tanned.

Stance: About to take off somewhere else.

Dress: Wears sporty or casual clothes that favour comfort and action and may look thrown on at the last minute.

Favourite Word: Why?

Says: Who, what, why, when, how, but.

Never says: Let's stay put.

Career: Teacher, lawyer, travel agent, philosopher, tutor, personal trainer, interpreter, public relations consultant, bookseller.

Archetype: The Questioner.

Shadow: The Pathological Liar.

Likes: Travel, freedom and wide open spaces. Some like sport, most like the outdoor life. Archery, racing, reading, studying languages, philosophy, partying.

Dislikes: Being tied down, repetition, routine or boredom.

Money: Spend, spend, spend.

Dreams: Of finding the ultimate answer.

Getting to know Sagittarius

Personality style: I am enthusiastic, sociable and boisterous, liking company when exploring the world but I can thrive alone. A born adventurer.

Optimistic and outgoing and always on the move, I'm the eternal student on a quest for knowledge. Blunt and tactless and prone to exaggeration with devastating frankness I tell it like it is. Not for me the little white lies that avoid hurt, things are said unwrapped. I want to be straightforward in my dealings with people, preferring truth and openness. Until that is there is something I would rather someone else didn't know. I can be somewhat economical with the truth but, not being a good liar, find it impossible to keep up the pretence for long, the truth will out. I'm a happy-go-lucky, uncomplicated sign and 'what you see is what you get' – unless you give your protagonist a complex moon-sign. I'm impulsive and I tend to loose off my arrows at random, acting first and thinking later. A naturally trusting person, I have faith in everyone – until I'm proved wrong. Please note, I hate being lied to. If someone does lie, while I may give them a second chance they will never be fully trusted again and ultimately I move smartly on.

What makes Sagittarius tick: "Never explain and never apologise' is my credo and I rarely look back with regret. I have an insatiable need to know and pursue this knowledge relentlessly, which is why I value my freedom so highly. Whilst happy to stay voluntarily, the thought of being tied down is extremely difficult for me. Wise partners give me lots of space. They recognise that even the most exciting plans become boring to me if they have been made too far in advance. There are always so many possibilities. I much prefer to fire all my arrows in the air at once and see where that leads. Like most Sagittarians I've got lofty ideals, I need something to inspire me and something to believe in. Given a cause, I can become quite fanatical and give my all but I have a tendency to promise more than can possibly be delivered, from the best of motives of course.'

The Sagittarian shadow: My continual need to know can become obsessive and I can be high maintenance mentally. Boredom is feared more than anything. I hate to be overlooked or to have nothing to do and when bored I become positively lethal. I'm prone to throwing over responsibilities and moving on regardless despite the broken promises that will litter the ground behind me. Other people accuse me of being insincere, unreliable and cutting. I'm the sort of character who needs adventure and challenge. I'm much more interesting that way. Like Walter Mitty I can inhabit a world created entirely by my own fantasies. I make an excellent conman and enjoy a flutter. You shouldn't believe all you hear about me though. I'm a master of disinformation when I want to be.

Sagittarian speak: 'Yes those dates are all ok for me although I may not make the May one as I should be in or on the way to Budapest but I'm trying to move that trip back so I can go to the Megalithomania weekend. In which case, I'll be with you that Thursday. I'm due in Manchester the following week.' [An email from me to my writing group organiser]

Your Sagittarius male character

What you most need to know about me is that I will not be tied down. Domesticity is not my bag, although if you give me freedom I happily stay around, and I might even fill the dishwasher occasionally. I'm much more likely to take on chores or choices if I think it's my idea. I'm quite easily manipulated that way. I'm frank and tactless. I'm not trying to hurt anyone, I'm telling it like it is. If someone asks: "Does my bum look big in this?" they have to be prepared for an uncompromising "Yes!" You can rely on me to be truthful, unless I have something to hide or a hidden agenda. If I do, you'll probably guess, I'm an incompetent liar. My body language gives it away, I wriggle and refuse to make eye contact, and I inevitably let it out in one of those foot-in-mouth moments I'm prone to. I need to debate and question and enquire. I'm the eternal student, whether of love, philosophy or material facts. What keeps me a lively and enter-taining companion is the opportunity to explore new things. This means that I take up a new activity with great enthusiasm, only to quickly drop it again so please don't comment! It also means that I have a huge circle of good friends of both sexes with whom I can enjoy life but I soon drop anyone who makes too many emotional demands on me. I don't understand jealousy and I'm not averse to sex with friends. The most important thing to remember about me is that I cannot stand to be bored. My sign becomes positively lethal when mired in routine, so plan some surprises to keep our writing relationship fresh and lively. Improvise, give me plenty of space, join in my adventures and be a stimulating companion on life's journey.

Your Sagittarius female character

I have no qualms about revealing myself to you in one explosive burst. I'm an up-front, freedom-loving kind of woman. Quickly bored and, in some cases, very competitive, I tend to use sport or outdoor activities to mop up my excess energy, but there are times when I want to release this in the bedroom. At such times I need raw sex without too many preliminaries. In another mood, I want to be wooed romantically and taken on a trip. But you won't have to worry I'll make my demands abundantly clear. I'm a lady who knows her own mind. Give me plenty of space, make sure I always have a case packed and another adventure in mind, another place to go, another idea to explore, and we'll have an enthusiastic writing relationship.

Love style: I'm passionate but not totally committed. For me, the grass could be greener someplace else.

I'm a free spirit who roams the world in search of adventure. My attitude to relationships is casual, I'll happily have a quick fling, or a mad, passionate affair that lasts months; I might move in with my lover as long as there is tempestuous sex and plenty of freedom to be myself, but eventually I'll probably want to move on. Marriage is not my ideal state. I'm never quite convinced that I have found my life partner. A romantic at heart, and someone who spontaneously shows affection, I often think I've found true love but I confuse it with a passing lust. Happiest with a partner who allows me the space I need, and who is delighted to pack a suitcase and accompany me on my latest trip, I seldom travel alone for long.

What Sagittarius seeks: I'm looking for adventure, hot sex, space and freedom, an accommodating relationship and possibly marriage.

Seduction technique: I'm an adventurous sign and I like a challenge. I enjoy the thrill of the chase as much as the hot sex that follows. But I'm not tenacious. If someone plays too hard to get, I simply move onto the next possibility. Impulsive and feisty, I often confuse love with infatuation, and have sexual encounters for fun and friendship as well as lust.

Flirting: I flirt with my mind and sometimes forget to include my body so it may not be obvious that I am flirting. To be truthful, I'm usually much more interested in what people have to say.

Trust and intimacy: I'm a naturally trusting person until it proves otherwise. Intimacy, I'm not sure. I'll share my thoughts with you. Will that do?

Secret sexual desire: Well it used to be joining the Mile High Club but too many people became members so now it's having sex on – or possibly with – Jupiter.

Sagittarius as a partner

Partnership style I seek a partner who understands and shares my need for freedom and adventure.

So long as my lover doesn't demand eternal fidelity, I'll probably be faithful. Given sufficient space, I can be a reasonably committed and caring partner – albeit one who finds the state of matrimony restricting. If I feel trapped I may leave for a time, but I can be a surprisingly loyal partner who forgives foibles and lapses on the part of others provided that they are honest and I have not been lied to (or you haven't given me a moon-sign that countermands this). My happy go lucky nature extends into my partnership arrangements and some signs see me as lacking in responsibility just because, if asked to do the shopping, I forget the staples and bring home the goodies. I've got the same attitude to bills. I'd much rather my partner took over dull routine tasks. I surprise my lover with spur of the moment outings. I forget to consult my lover's diary first, expecting him or her to drop whatever plans had been made to be with me. If there are objections, I cannot understand why. After all, life is for living, isn't it? If my partner turns the tables on me, I gladly go along, provided I haven't anything more interesting in mind. I'm not likely to put my own life on hold to fit into my partner's.

What Sagittarius expects from a partner: I need my partner to communicate with me. A strong silent type drives me to distraction. If I can't discuss things, I lose my vitality. I need a tolerant, non-possessive partner. I expect a partner to allow me freedom to roam, being kept on a short leash brings out the worst in me. Don't expect me to always be there. Twenty-four hour togetherness is just not my style – unless we're travelling. It's not that I want to be unfaithful, just that I need to explore other possibilities and to have time for hobbies and friends and I'd prefer that my partner did too. That way, when we come back to the relationship, our interest is renewed.

When a relationship ends: By the time a relationship ends conclusively I have already breathed a sigh of relief and left. As far as I am concerned, that is that. It only remains to tie up the legal niceties, and I'm none too bothered about those. I'm quite capable of walking out with nothing and starting from scratch – again.

Sagittarius as a friend

Friendship Style: I'm gregarious, bright, breezy and spontaneous.

I make a great friend. Gregarious, endlessly curious and enthusiastic, and very, very lively, I'll party the night away, debate into the small hours, have long lunches, or jump on a plane with your character. The spending capacity of my sign is legendary so I'm just the person for a spot of retail therapy, if there is room on your character's credit card. I won't even check the balance on mine. The same applies when it's time to take a holiday, your protagonist is guaranteed to boldly go where no tourist has been before. I like to be surrounded by mates and I enjoy team sports. I've always got an opinion to air, so your character had better be ready with some pithy retort. I don't get on with people who don't have ideas of their own. When it comes to a crisis, I'm incredibly resourceful. My advice is sage, if sometimes somewhat impractical, and I do not panic easily. If your character's angst is emotional, I'll spend hours discussing all the intimate details, I'm fascinated by what makes other people tick. Just don't expect me to empathise sloppily though, feelings aren't my thing. And, remember, your character will get total honesty. If your character's talking to me in confidence, swear me to secrecy. I can be a bit of a blabbermouth.

Sagittarius as a co-worker

Co-worker Style: I'm hard working but not too dedicated.

I'm a gregarious co-worker. Colleagues are inevitably assimilated into my circle of friends and the boundaries between work and social life blur. I rarely keep personal matters to myself. I share all the joys and problems of my life, whether your character wants me to or not. Finally, we get down to business. I'm a past master at displacement activities but these create thinking time. I'm full of sparky ideas and good intentions. I'm always happy to help out. Where I might fall down is on delivery. I'm prone to take on far too much. Somehow I forget the time things take and get bored. Wise co-workers check my schedules carefully.

By the light of the adventurous moon

The Sagittarius moon: I'm companionable and optimistic with a fund of wisdom to draw on. Just don't rely on me.

I'm the courtesan moon: charming, intelligent, entertaining and, although I'm excellent in bed, non-committal and emotionally detached. My independent Moon tends to speak its mind and some other signs find it difficult to face my relentless honesty, but when this is tempered with humour and kindness it provides powerful insights – it all depends on the sun-sign I am paired with. My quest for knowledge never ceases. In the past I learned how to detach from my emotions and may well use words to create an emotional block rather than actually feel my feelings. I'm driven by a desire for emotional freedom. Truth is a powerful need, I've been misled in the past and I instinctively know when I am being lied to. I act impulsively and intuitively, and then may regret my actions. I dislike emotional demands and any form of neediness, which means that I move on rather than deal with issues, forever chasing my dream. Like-mindedness nurtures me.

Meeting the world

The Sagittarius mask: Questioning and questing.

The number of questions I ask is the first thing other people notice about me. I often put my foot in my mouth, I can't help it, words just pop out regardless of whether it's appropriate or not. I have a kind of verbal Tourette's but without the swearing or tics. When your character puts me on to face the world we'll be flying out of the door. One of the great adventurers of the zodiac, I've always got somewhere new to be, a quest to fulfil, a question to answer, and a fund of wisdom to draw on. I act on the spur of the moment and speak my mind with relentless honesty. Although I can help even the most honest of sun-signs out with convenient little white lies if necessary. I'm an indefatigable traveller and usually have a bag packed 'just in case'. I don't hide behind a mask, I merely move on. I can be haphazard to say the least. But I have the knack of coming up with some great ideas, and innovative solutions.

Sagittarius compatibility rating

Aries *****; Taurus **; Gemini *****; Cancer *; Leo *****; Virgo**; Libra *****; Scorpio *; Sagittarius *****; Capricorn *; Aquarius****; Pisces*

Chapter 15

Capricorn
The Goat

♑ **22 December – 19 January**

The lust of the goat is the bounty of God.
William Blake (Sagittarius sun, Cancer moon and rising)

Crib sheet

First impression: Serious, Capricorns look like they can be relied upon.

Appearance: Long, lean and bony. There is a certain greyness to Capricorn, hair often turns grey prematurely.

Stance: Authoritative, facial expression may be severe.

Dress: Stylish clothes even when casual but colours tend to be somewhat colourless, dark and conservative.

Favourite Word: Should.

Says: Seriously. Ought. Obey.

Never says: Anything without deliberating first.

Career: Businessman, finance officer, comedy writer, judge, lawmaker, politician, bureaucrat, government worker, pensions administrator, orthopaedic surgeon, insurance salesman, magistrate, custody sergeant.

Archetype: The conservative.

Shadow: Narrow-minded control freak.

Likes: Certainty and order, black comedy, hill walking, climbing, marathon running, yoga, golf, wine-tasting, genealogy, gardening, d.i.y., reading biographies, museums, wine-buff.

Dislikes: Chaos, inefficiency, being coerced.

Money: Equals authority and security, tends to be tight-fisted.

Dreams: Of controlling the world.

Getting to know Capricorn

Personality style: I am confident, authoritarian, commanding, humorous, and a control freak.

I belong to a very serious sign, which can lead to being a strict disciplinarian. But fortunately I'm enlivened by a black sense of humour and a finely honed sense of the absurd. I also have a great deal of wisdom to impart. With my strong sense of responsibility and duty, old age is usually happier for me than youth. Other people accuse me of being overly conventional and narrow minded, hidebound by rules and regulations. But I just want to stick with what is right. I pay great attention to material matters until my security is assured, and can be extremely ambitious. But then I turn to more spiritual matters. I have an innate struggle between authority and authoritarianism. Caution and inhibition go along with great resilience and strength of character. I'm concerned with keeping to the rules, doing my duty and maintaining the status quo. I learn control and continence early in life and climb the ladder of ambition with determination. I am sober and responsible – while I'm young. As I mature, I become much lighter hearted, growing into my wisdom. Lecherous old age suits me rather well. I have a hard time trying to live up to the tough standards I set for myself and the expectations society has of me. I'd like to loosen up and practise the art of 'live and let live' but I find that hard until I'm too old for it to matter. There is a marked difference between the male and female denizens of my sign, more so than with any other side of the zodiac.

What makes Capricorn tick: I was born with a sense of having a job to do, a burden to bear, something to achieve which was difficult when I was young because I didn't have the clout. As I mature I grow into my role but I still feel inadequate to the task of doing my duty. Male or female, I often have to play the role of father early in life, supporting the family. I want to make a difference to society. Valuing home and family, I adhere to strict rules and conventional mores but I'm a surprisingly assertive sign when it comes to taking charge. I need to be a success. I cannot be swayed by spurious arguments or sob-stories. I'm definitely not a soft touch.

The Capricorn shadow: I feel overwhelmed by responsibility and anything inconvenient that doesn't fit into my sign's world view is carefully quarantined into a corner of my mind. Other signs accuse me of being a control freak but I'm terrified of anarchy so I've become a tyrant. My negative emotional programming has induced a deeply pessimistic approach to life and I suffer from destructive depressions. I embrace authoritarianism, rigid beliefs and extreme judgemental intolerance. Bigotry, narrow mindedness, and self-righteousness seem to come naturally to me. I hold onto the past at all costs. Any crime I commit is going to involve having power over large numbers of people, or powering my way to the top. I'd make an excellent crime boss.

Capricorn speak: 'Please don't think me cavalier (no one uses that word any more or do they) but every day I have some commitment – so often an earnest commitment. Although when it's cold outside, and one is semi-tired and longing to lie in the bath munching apples and reading, even frivolous commitments don't appeal.' Sue Joiner (Capricorn sun), email to Village Writers.

Your Capricorn male character

You'll find me difficult to get to know – and even harder to understand. Perhaps I need to teach you a little more astrology before we go any further. I belong to a 'negative' – that is, feminine, receptive sign – but one that's ruled over by the bleakest, coldest, hardest and most masculine planet, Saturn. Saturn has to do with boundaries and convention, rules and regulations so it's no wonder I'm conflicted and addicted to structure and control. I desperately want my life to be well ordered and secure. Without this anchor I feel scarily vulnerable and, with stern taskmaster Saturn wagging an admonitory finger, I'll do anything to hold onto my authority. You'll have to gently encourage me to unburden my soul if you want to get to the heart of my character. I don't find introspection easy, so I rarely know what I am feeling and I am uncomfortable with raw emotion. I am cut off from the receptive, intuitive side of my nature. You have to understand that I constantly seek validation from the outside world. I need the top job, big house, executive car and trophy wife to feel that I've made it and yet I am at my most comfortable within the family unit. I take my responsibilities very seriously indeed. But Saturn also has innate wisdom. Think of me as a wise mentor. Black moods descend on me suddenly and obliterate everything else. It is no good trying to jolly me along, it simply won't work. Give me a safe, contained space and it passes. Sometimes my satirical black sense of humour helps. Monty Pythonesque, I see the funny side of misfortune and enjoy slapstick and satire.

Your Capricorn female character

I'm more in touch with my earthy sensual nature than my male counterpart, and more receptive to what life brings. I find it easier to ebb and flow, not demanding so much control, although I need to feel safe and secure. Don't you dare go all sentimental on me. I'd prefer it if you didn't show strong emotions when I'm around. I can't cope. I may opt for the apparent security of marriage to an older man, a "sugar daddy" who fulfils my material rather than emotional needs, or put marriage aside in favour of getting a top job. I'm introspective and can find the inner approval that takes me away from my constant childhood-induced need to be looked on with favour by the world. Exploring my strengths and accepting my weaknesses compassionately, I channel my sense of duty with more kindness to myself than I do to others. That doesn't mean I feel any less accountable, however. It's just that I've realised I cannot be responsible for policing the world – although I take pleasure in locking up villains where I can. I need something to believe in beyond the shackles of conventional religion, something which takes me to the highest part of my being and which helps me to find my own inner authority and power.

Capricorn in love

Love style: I'm conventional, faithful, inhibited and supportive.

I find it hard to be physically demonstrative and I hate talking about my feelings. I'm told it's the influence of repressive Saturn that creates my emotional inhibitions. I recognise that I may appear to be cold and forbidding even when I've fallen deeply in love – and I often hide how I feel because I don't feel worthy of love. I just don't know what to do about it. Intimacy is a stranger to me and I'd hate to make a mistake. It is not that I do not have an affectionate nature, I do, but physical expression of how I'm feeling puts me under the scrutiny of judgemental Saturn. Fortunately I've found that, paradoxically, I become increasingly light hearted and more affectionate the older I get. In the second half of life, I really get the hang of relationships and emotional interchange. Given the right partner, my earthy sexuality comes to the fore and I throw off my inhibitions, although I still find it somewhat difficult to express myself emotionally or to believe that I deserve a happy life.

What Capricorn seeks: I'm looking for security, regular sex, commitment, loyalty and marriage.

Seduction technique: I'm serious about most things and satisfying my sex drive is no exception but, at heart, I'm looking for the security of a lasting relationship and tend to equate lust with love. When I set out to seduce I show my chilly charm but fear of failure holds me back. My sexual target may feel that he or she is being assessed for suitability rather than seduced. It is only when I get to bed that the lecherous goat emerges.

Flirting: Me flirt? Well, yes, I suppose I do sometimes when I feel safe and secure. I use humour and wit, I find that works best.

Trust and intimacy: I'm closed and mistrustful. Intimacy does not come easily to me.

Secret sexual desire: I crave domination and being swept off my feet by ungovernable passion.

Capricorn as a partner

Partnership style: I'm not comfortable with public shows of affection so my behaviour around a partner is somewhat formal.

I am solid and dependable, with a deep commitment to my partner. I do not go in for hand holding or smoochy moments unless I'm in the privacy of my own home. Spontaneous gestures are not for me and I am more likely to buy someone a present to show how fond I am of them than to tell them so. I'm deeply ambitious and hardworking, so my partner may complain I put business before pleasure. It is important to me to keep my status-symbol home well supplied with material goods. I am capable of romantic gestures such as presenting a diamond ring as we dine *a deux* in an expensive restaurant, accompanied by an excellent bottle of wine. Initially cautious and mistrustful of a lover, once I am committed I want to spend all my spare time with my partner and work at ensuring that the relationship runs smoothly. However, I have control issues that I cannot put aside. I need to be the one in charge, to be looked up to in the relationship, to be master in my home and to be obeyed. I don't enjoy a totally equal partnership and a wise partner allows me to have the illusion, if not the reality, of being head of the household.

What Capricorn expects from partners: Loyalty, fidelity, conformity and obedience come high on my list of requirements from a partner. I want someone who looks well groomed and who never lets me down in public. In private, it is a different matter. I need a considerate lover who gently unfurls my formidable sexuality, someone who can make me behave like the horny goat I was born to be.

When it ends: Gloom pervades my life and I do all I can to string the connection out, even if I am the one to leave. Divorce equals failure and I don't like to admit to mistakes. If I do leave, I feel extremely responsible and ensure that those left behind are provided for. If I was the one who was left, I want my material security well covered in the divorce. It's my right after all.

Capricorn as a friend

Friendship Style: I'm committed, serious and attentive.

As a friend, I'm dependable, loyal and practical. While I have no time for emotional angst, I am incredibly well organised and can sort your character's life out in a trice. The advice will be down to earth and pragmatic. Your character's lover is causing anguish? Leave! – with a financial settlement of course. Your character needs somewhere to live? Get a mortgage – I place great faith in bricks and mortar and see these as a symbol of worldly success. If your character has money worries, I'll soon have these sorted, and your character talked into a pension plan and insurance for everything you can think of along the way. My friends remind me that all work and no play makes Jack, or Jill, very dull indeed. It could be a good idea to organise something on a regular basis. I like to join in worthy activities especially those geared towards the good of the community, but a trip to the mountains may be just what I need. One thing that may surprise your character is my black sense of humour. Although I perceive life as full of gloom and responsibility, I am able to keep things in perspective by laughing at the ridiculousness of it all.

Capricorn as a co-worker

Co-worker Style: I'm serious, committed, utterly reliable and frighteningly ambitious.

I am too ambitious to be content with being a co-worker for long. Highly organised and efficient, I'd better be in charge. I want to boost to my authority and will not tolerate being under-mined in any way. I demand respect and work best in a situation of mutual cooperation although I quite naturally gravitate to a position of power, chairing meetings and so on. If your character is able to tolerate this, then our work relationship runs smoothly, and a great deal is achieved. I defuse tension with a witty remark. I never slack on the job and expect everyone else to show the same dedication to duty as I cannot tolerate incompetence of any kind. Your character will get the best out of working with me if I'm not hurried, flustered or challenged. Let me think it was my own idea.

By the light of the authoritarian moon

Capricorn moon style: I'm a diligent, responsible moon whose urge is towards doing what is right and to being useful to society. **Basic need:** control.

Although I'm cautious, I have innate authority and I'm used to being obeyed. I care deeply about people and work for their best interests. Other people see me as tightly controlled and emotionally cool, repressed even. Deep down, I feel cut off and unloved, and unable to express my feelings. I tend to sublimate my emotional needs into material things, or into reaching the top. And yet I long for deep emotional connection with others. I know that loving myself is an essential preliminary to accepting love from other people but I find this tough. I've got an inferiority complex and am prone to melancholy and deep despair with a fear of being judged and found lacking. The old tapes that subconsciously run me are full of 'oughts' and 'shoulds', rules and regulations, what I ought to be thinking or believing, what I should be doing. I've internalised all the authoritarian voices from my past. I'd be much freer if I could tune into the voice of my own self. I don't want your pity but much of my childhood lacked affection or warmth, and I was only approved of if I conformed to family expectations. I feel overwhelmed with responsibilities and limitations. I know I would be nurtured by loving and accepting myself. Underneath, I'm an intuitive person with great wisdom.

Meeting the world

The Capricorn mask: I come with burdens, baggage and Things To Do.

When your character puts me on to face the world it's a pretty serious business. I am somewhat gloomy and pessimistic and need to conform. My mask is one of strict control, an authoritarian face devoted to the 'oughts and shoulds' of life. This sternness can disguise a much freer sun-sign, giving your character a hard time, and causing other people to view me as cold and critical. I do have an air of authority. I was born 'old'. I have a strongly developed sense of responsibility, I feel that there is a task I must do, a burden to carry. As I mature, I'm determined to reach the top. I organise other people's lives as well as my own and enforce 'rules'. Strong powers of leadership were bestowed at my birth but my ruler, Saturn, is a hard task master. I was also given self-discipline and a desire to put my inherent wisdom to use in the world. Although there may seem to be no way out, I can turn a crisis into a challenge and find my innate strength.

Capricorn compatibility rating

Aries ****; Taurus *****; Gemini *; Cancer *****; Leo *; Virgo ****; Libra ****; Scorpio **; Sagittarius *; Capricorn *****; Aquarius *; Pisces **

Chapter 16

Aquarius
The Water Bearer

♒ **21 January – 18 February**

And even since I have seen you I have endeavoured often 'to reason against the reason of my Love'.
John Keats (Scorpio sun, Gemini moon)

Crib sheet

First impression: Cool.

Appearance: Hair is wiry and misshapen teeth are a facial characteristic.

Stance: Wired or deep in thought. Frequently appears to be observing humanity from a distance.

Dress: Aquarius likes to be different; often bizarre and eccentric, startling or hippy. May wear bright, electric colours or black. Outfits are outrageous, high fashion or highly individual – thrift shop chic.

Favourite Word: Revolutionise.

Says: What do we need for the future? Have you ever thought of … ? Have you tried … ?"

Never says: Look at the past.

Career: Quantum physicist, systems analyst, buyer, sociologist, technologist, charity worker, futures trader, complementary medicine, psychologist, campaigner.

Archetype: The revolutionary.

Shadow: The anarchist.

Likes: Being different, internet sex, innovative technology, anything quirky, chaos and instability, racquet sports, skiing, dancing, UFO-watching, computers, charitable work, protesting, science fiction and comics.

Dislikes: Rules and regulations, dull conformity.

Money: Spends on the bizarre and eccentric.

Dreams: Of changing the world.

The Aquarius personality

Personality style: Revolutionary crossed with mad professor, a quirky personality always ahead of its time. A natural outsider.

I was born before my time. I'm a genius and a misfit, a highly original and inventive visionary who is misunderstood by the rest of humanity which is why I'm also a rebel. One of the movers and shakers of society. Although I am extremely articulate about where humanity is going and what it is doing to itself I find it incredibly difficult to express my feelings about anything personal or intimate. A social conscience and concern for humanity drive me forward, I want to bring in revolution to overturn the status quo, and I have a deep desire to improve the future. I believe in equality for all. I inhabit the brave new world of possibilities, coming back into the present moment is a challenge I do not relish.

What makes Aquarius tick: Perverse and unpredictable, I am a sign that simply has to be different. On principle, I never do what

I'm expected to do and yet I can get stuck in the most eccentric rut. My sign has two planets in charge, Saturn, the most conventional planet in the zodiac and Uranus, the most unpredictable. These two battle it out in my psyche and, when an irresistible force meets an immovable object, chaos results. But I can be a great catalyst for change. I don't belong on this earth and yet I am desperately concerned for its future. I get on with humanity as a whole better than in one-to-one situations. I sometimes feel like a scientist peering in at a laboratory experiment trying to understand what makes people tick. Well-meaning friends tell me this is because I am cut off from my feelings. I know that I intensely dislike emotional messiness, encouraging others to follow my example and rise above irrational feelings into rational objectivity. But on the other hand, I am endlessly fascinated by the human condition. My conundrum is to uncork the emotions locked within myself.

The Aquarian Shadow: Fanaticism and bigotry run deep in me. I'm a chaotic anarchist at heart. Off with the old and on with the new! Saturn points his finger and tells how it should be. But Uranus comes along and throws it all up in the air. If I can't get my vision of the future in place any other way I happily start a revolution. If I'm going to turn to crime it will have technology and science at its core. I might use biological warfare or take over the internet. Let's create a perfect world – my way.

Aquarius speak: '"To make a difference, we must be different". Aquarian Abraham Lincoln said something along those lines – having the willingness to stand out, go against the grain, dance like no-one is watching, and love like it's never going to hurt. Aquarians seem to have a way of being themselves regardless of what others think of them. And as we enter the mystery of this zodiacal perspective, our work is to release that freedom of expression that flies in the face of social convention and throws a spanner of works of the rules of etiquette and decorum.' John Wadsworth, Aquarian astrologer and workshop leader (http://www.thealchemicaljourney.co.uk)

Your Aquarius male character: You don't write me. I desperately want to maintain my individuality, and do exactly the opposite of what you wish simply to make the point that I stand alone. A catalyst for change, I'm a complex man and an unpredictable one. Attuned to technology and innovation, I'm designing the new world right now. What you see is definitely not all there is. I appear to be insensitive because of my emotional disconnection but I am acutely sensitive to subtle nuances of mood and behaviour. I find it extremely difficult to open up and tell you how I feel so you have to intuit this for yourself. To be frank, I have a problem. Somewhere in the depths of my being, I'm seeking a soulmate to make me feel I have come home. Of course, I never tell you this, or if I do I argue the case for soulmates with cynical and dispassionate rationality. But secretly, in my romantic heart, I believe there is someone out there, a one-off, a one and only, twin soul. If I find her, I'll never let go. In all areas of my life I face a dilemma. Should I live within the limits Saturn sets, or bring about the transformation that revolutionary Uranus is urging? I can be meticulous, or wildly eccentric and totally out of control. The problem for you is that one can easily masquerade as the other. Give me space, and remember that intimacy and commitment are alien territory to me.

Your Aquarius female character

I often feel like I've landed here from another planet and am still trying to understand this world. I remain tantalizingly out of your reach as making an emotional connection is problematic for me, becoming intimate even more so. I am likely to do, or say, the most bizarre things and wise writers learn to leave it, I am not being personal. I did not mean to insult anyone it just came out that way. I am abrupt, tactless and unconventional, but I have a sensitive soul underneath who needs to feel loved and who, once I have committed, is loyal for ever. I take pleasure in the bizarre and unusual aspects of life and I'm always looking to the future. In fact, I'm busy right now setting the year after next year's trends and I'm not afraid to take on the establishment. I'm a protestor here to challenge the status quo and fight for humanity, a Greenham Common woman at heart. In the past I happily camped outside the airfield gates until the nuclear missiles left but before they'd gone I'd turned my mind to the next worthy campaign. Freeing Tibet is definitely on my agenda.

Aquarius in love

Love style: Decidedly different.

I've got strong passions although I find it difficult to connect to them. I intellectualise, discuss and rarely recognise that I'm motivated by lust and emotion. I enjoy experimenting with sex, but actually feeling the feelings perplexes me. I ask myself: "What is this thing called love?" I am perfectly capable of being in love with an unattainable person but having a relationship with someone who is available in the meantime. When I do find a partner, outside the bedroom I am coolly affectionate although I may surprise my partner with a romantic gesture or with wild sex in unexpected places. I need personal space and I do like to do things differently.

Aquarius seeks: casual sex, mental stimulation, companionship, the unconventional, possibly marriage.

Seduction technique: My aloof sexual style is one of contrariness and contrast. I positively crackle with electricity which can be exciting for my potential lovers, and yet there is little connection with my dispassionate head so I don't always act on the signals my body, or a prospective lover, send me, and if I do, it may be over in a flash. Then, on the other hand, I can be romantic and sweetly seductive. It all depends on the whim of the moment.

Flirting: I often find what goes on in my head a much greater turn on than anything someone else may do, so my flirting tends to be cool and aloof, playing mind games and weaving a web of words around the object of my interest just to see what the response is.

Trust and intimacy: I'm detached and dispassionate.

Secret sexual desire: kinky sex amid emotional meltdown.

Aquarius as a partner

Partnership style: As I tend not to be bound by conventions, and hate to be bored, I am likely to have an unconventional set up.

I'm free spirited and value my individuality, finding intimacy challenging, but I nevertheless yearn for a settled relationship. When I find one, I either stick with it no matter how bad, or I suddenly leave for no specific reason. As a partner, I can be something of an enigma. Rather than emotional connection, I want a meeting of minds. Always fair minded, I give equal value to the uniqueness of my partner. I am supportive of my partner's personal growth. I enjoy rationally discussing progress and am objective if issues come up that I can assist with. I have the knack of helping someone rise up out of the mire into the light of a new awareness but I'm baffled by a complete emotional meltdown and start analysing the situation far too soon, or so I'm told. If my partner demands fidelity, I look to the future. Not that I necessarily leave, but I make the point that I cannot be tied down. I am an extremely loyal and faithful lover once I've found what I'm looking for. I have difficulty with intimacy and yet secretly I want stability so finding the right partner is a great relief to me, although I still take things step by step and wait for my partner to commit first. Until that time, I hold myself aloof, finding an outlet for my sexual urges without getting too involved so I have flings and fantasies and I may play out my freedom-commitment dilemma through free-love or a f***-buddy.

What Aquarius expects from a partner: Whatever the next sexual trend is going to be, I have already been there so I need a partner who is prepared to experiment sexually and with different types of relationships. Intellectual companionship is vital and I want a partner who shares my interest in what makes humanity tick, and who is prepared to do something about the state of the world. I like my partner to be around when I want company, and elsewhere the remainder of the time. My personal space is important to me and I may prefer to occupy separate houses. A partner who has plenty of outside interests and a supportive group of friends is ideal, particularly as I refuse to get involved in my partner's emotional angst. I might not mind the odd lover or two, there is not a conventional bone in my body, so Aquarians have some rather strange arrangements by other sign's standards. What I do not forgive is a partner who tries to take my individuality away although I may gladly surrender it.

When a relationship ends: Endings are difficult for my contradictory sign. I am fixed and yet unpredictable, prone to throwing the baby out with the bathwater. I could up and leave everything, or hold on at all costs, but I will have planned it carefully. In many ways, it is easier for me if my partner is the one to go. At least I know where I stand.

Aquarius as a friend

Friendship style: dispassionate, formal.

I enjoy friendship because emotional intimacy is not required. I am a gregarious sign so I like being part of a crowd. Or rather,

I people-watch and that happens best in a crowd although I stand slightly aloof. I am a shrewd observer of human nature. But your character needs to remember that there will be times when I need my space. I'm the person to take on a shopping trip for the future or to book a spaceship to Mars. I have an excellent eye for innovative design or the latest technology and give wise advice. I'm a patient teacher and a staunch ally in a crisis. But your character shouldn't expect sympathy, after a peremptory "Sorry about that" I help your character move out of misery and into an objective assessment of the situation. With my shrewd mind it won't be long before your character's problem is solved. If your character's heart is broken, you'll have to look elsewhere for TLC, but his or her personal life is sorted. And if you want to do something different, I'm the friend to talk to. Aquarians celebrate the uniqueness of everyone.

Aquarius as a co-worker
Co-worker style: self-contained, workaholic.

I'm something of a contradiction as a co-worker, a combination of the shrewd with the intuitive, the rational with the leap of faith. I'm friendly enough and keenly absorbed in the work provided it is intellectually challenging or socially rewarding, and I can work well as part of a team, but, and it is a big but, I belong to an individualistic sign that wants to do things my way. It can be useful to listen to my suggestions, my innovative mind is keenly attuned to the next new thing, the trend that will hit in five years' time, the invention that will save the planet and so on. Make a note of all my bizarre ideas, they work! Patent them as in a few years they'll be all the rage. If you give me space an Aquarius in the business could be excellent news. If you don't, it could get chaotic.

By the light of the eccentric moon

Aquarius Moon style: cut off and remote.

Basic need: space.

I'm an original one of a kind, eccentric and independent, self-contained, with a flair for social science. Deeply concerned about the future of the planet, I have enormous potential for expressing universal love if only I can find the way. I stay emotionally objective, unswayed by arguments that tug at the heartstrings. My desire is to facilitate social change and the evolution of humankind. I'm stuck in an old pattern of rebellion and wilfulness, part of my personality tends automatically to do the opposite of whatever is suggested, and I never obey instructions, I have a strong need for emotional independence and yet I feel cut off and isolated. I've been told I'm commitment-phobic. When challenged by relationships, I retreat into a cold and lonely place. My aloofness and desire for independence can lead to loneliness and erratic behaviour, which I know needs to be brought under my conscious control. I am run by a powerful old tape that centres round rebellion and change. My emotions swing wildly and they frighten me. I need closure. To be honest, I feel as though a spaceship dropped me off on earth and I've been waiting for it to come back ever since. I know if I could alleviate my feelings of alienation it would bring deep soul healing and I'd be welcomed into the brotherhood of humanity.

Meeting the world

The Aquarius mask: Your character doesn't so much put me on to meet the world as to peer down through it with scientific detachment.

I find it difficult to fit into society. The Aquarius mask is often zany and eccentric but is equally likely to be remote and aloof. I'm a far-sighted observer at heart. But show me a revolution waiting to happen and I'll poke it into life. When your character has me for a mask we're light years ahead of the rest of the world. I identify today what the world will need tomorrow, which makes for an excellent innovator and trendsetter. I want to promote the brotherhood of humanity and work for its good – and many of my solutions are revolutionary. This brings me into conflict with more conventionally minded people. Either your character adapts, and feels inwardly rebellious, or is the rebel who inwardly wants to conform, depending on the sun sign. My stubbornness and desire to be different makes me stand out from the crowd, but this may cover deep insecurity depending on the sun-sign. I know that what I think today, the world will be clamouring for tomorrow. If your character is trying to hide behind a mask of conformity, bring me on!

Aquarius compatibility rating:

Aries *****; Taurus ***; Gemini****; Cancer***; Leo*****; Virgo***; Libra ****; Scorpio***; Sagittarius***; Capricorn*; Aquarius*****; Pisces*

Chapter 17

Pisces
The Fishes

♓ **20 February – 20 March**

Sweet Love of youth, forgive,
If I forget thee, while the world's tide is bearing me along,
Other desires and other hopes beset me,
Hopes which obscure, but cannot do thee wrong!
Emily Bronte (Leo sun, Cancer moon)

Crib sheet:

First impression: Hypnotic.

Appearance: Fluid eyes gaze into another world. Face is expressive and alluring, body may be fleshy but Pisces exudes sexual attraction.

Stance: Languid and boneless.

Dress: Romantic.

Favourite Word: Love.

Says: Promise. I'll always love you.

Never says: No.

Career: Actor, dancer, poet, screenwriter, photographer, wine seller, artist, drug counsellor, pusher, hypnotherapist, nurse, priest, tarot reader, chiropodist, cruise director, fishmonger.

Archetype: The saviour.

Shadow: The victim.

Likes: Rose tinted glasses, religion, escapism, mysticism, making promises, film, art and theatre, water, photography, romantic dinners.

Dislikes: Harsh reality, dealing with detail and time constraints, truth.

Money: Slips away.

Dreams: Of escaping from the world.

The Pisces personality

Personality style: fluid, changeable and malleable.

You'll find when writing me that I'm difficult to pin down, the great escaper of the zodiac, I'm vague, dreamy and unfocused. I wish everyday life was more like what I see at the movies. Everyday reality is too harsh. I may appear to tell you everything, but I'll be hiding something as I want to be seen in the best possible light. I'm an incurable romantic but highly creative when I channel my passionate imagination. I'm compassionate and want to care for everyone, which leads me to take on tasks there is no possibility of fulfilling. I slip into saviour-rescuer-victim-martyr roles easily. Sadly people take advantage of me or I rescue the wrong person. They tell me that I can be manipulative and that I take liberties with truth. I'm such a sucker for a sob story. You'll enjoy writing me if you want a romantically conflicted character whose flaws and redeeming qualities almost balance each other out. Almost.

What Makes Pisces Tick: I really do want to save you and I can't help getting pulled into those rescuer, saviour, victim, martyr sub-plots. You never quite know where you are with me, but I don't know either. Other people think me naïve and gullible. Well perhaps I am. I'm deeply emotional and complex. Beneath the surface I'm pulled this way and that by currents and desires over which I have no control. If I can't understand myself, how can anyone else? I sometimes see parts of myself reflected back through other people's eyes but I find it hard to separate what is really me from what is them, especially as I intuitively feel what is going on inside them but cannot make rational sense of it. My boundaries are diffuse to say the least. I'm highly impressionable and cannot distinguish wishful thinking from what actually is, or you from me.

The Shadow: Oft-times the world is too harsh for my sensitive nature and I long for escape. The route can be through another person, a fantasy or a bottle. I sometimes unwittingly invite emotional abuse by my naïve trust of the bad guy or an unjustified confidence in my ability to reform. I simply cannot believe that it could happen again. Nor can I understand when people blame me even though I suffer from existential guilt and take the sins of the world upon my shoulders. People call me a psychic vampire. They say I manipulate and take advantage of their good nature. They say I never let go, that I don't listen and don't discriminate, I just live in my own world. I tend to turn to crime by accident, I promise so much and sometimes other people feel conned by my schemes and manoeuvrings. My lies and evasions are geared towards an easy life. I'd happily lose myself in you, why not you in me?

Pisces speak: 'What am I doing in Alexandria? A book prompted the journey, a library – the destination, and a revolution – the compulsion. I read Lawrence Durrell's Alexandria Quartet as a young woman, and it drew me to the city. Finally here I am, in a flat overlooking a traffic gorged Corniche and a sultry

Mediterranean. Lawrence Durrell's The Alexandria Quartet lies on a table. The book has been a lifetime companion, a nudging reminder of a dream. I first read the book as a young woman, seduced by the sexual and emotional charge of Durrell's city that mapped the terrain of the human heart in its 'thousand dust tormented streets.' His cosmopolitan characters seduced me as much as they seduced each other. Durrell said his Alexandria of the thirties and forties had gone forever. And now, a new city and a new Egypt beckons another generation of writers and readers. Is there anything of Durrell's Alexandria left to survive yet another revolution?' Christine Aziz: 'wordwhore and bookbitch' (Pisces sun) (http://www.wordsfromarevolution.com/)

Your Pisces male character

You've heard of the slippery fish ... well, just when you think you've achieved the impossible and understood me I swim off in another direction and you realise you haven't pinned me down at all. I effortlessly blend in to my surroundings and become whatever you want me to be – until someone else needs me. I react constantly to the subtle emotional stimuli I receive through my psychic antennae, intertwined with my own emotional desires. How can a writer expect to keep track of my fluid character? Let's see if I can help you. I have a soft heart and am easily taken in. I have two natures that swim in opposite directions. Whatever appears on the surface, something different is going on out of sight. I don't intend to spin webs of illusion and deceit, but I do, and suffer agonies of guilt and want to atone. My inner world is empathetic, emotional and, despite outward appearances, totally self-absorbed. I suffer terribly when I am disappointed. I need to be needed. For me, intimacy is all about emotional melding, becoming one. Creating physical, emotional and spiritual union. I tend to view life through the bottom of a bottle, it gives me the illusion of belonging. But other people will tell you I really am a different kind of slippery fish, one who can't be trusted, who promises everything but can't be caught, who lies and cheats his way through life. I'm not really sure what the truth is I've changed it so often and am adept at little white lies that just get bigger and bigger. It is hard to tell what is reality and what is fantasy. That's just how a Pisces is.

Your Pisces female character

I believe any tale I'm spun, especially if it makes me the centre of your world, but sadly it always leads to disillusionment or so it would seem, maybe next time I'll get it right? I do so want to be the heroine in my own drama. My taking on the emotional colouring of whatever surrounds me makes it pretty hard to actually get to know what is going on behind these big wide eyes of mine – especially when they're hidden behind rose-tinted glasses. You might sometimes get the feeling that it is all an act. I'm wildly imaginative and a brilliant actress so I can create whatever life I like for myself – for a little while at least. Unfortunately I'm frequently disappointed and hurt by life. People say I'm like a film star, sultry and lush, I cannot help turning on my magnets wherever I go and I leave a litter of broken hearts and shattered promises behind me. My whole body is awash with sexual excitement and promise no matter who I'm meeting. I swim in a river of deep emotions and intuitive impressions, and I rarely know how I really feel. I'd like you to reflect feelings back to me so that I can become more aware of them. Then perhaps I'll be able to understand myself. My romantic dreams leave me vulnerable and I often become the victim of my own illusions. No matter how many disappointments I have, naively trusting, I still have high hopes of my relationship with you. Please don't take advantage of me. Make me exciting, glamorous, like one of the old movie stars, and I'll love you forever.

Pisces in love

Love style: emotional melding.

Deeply sympathetic and compassionate, I have a strong desire to save my lover. When in saviour or rescuer mode, I have no discrimination. I give and give, and then find that I have flipped into the victim or martyr. I find myself asking: "What did I do to deserve this?" or saying "After all I've done for you ... ." I'm disappointed to find that the perfect love I thought I'd found is but another chapter in the old scenario. However, my forgiving nature rarely learns and I am taken advantage of over and over again. I live in the inner world of my imagination and my day dreams have substance for me. I fantasize about my one and only true soulmate, the perfect love affair. I step into myth and magic to find my fantasy partner and the problem lies in ascertaining which of my lovers is imaginary and which is real; so enamoured am I with love that I confuse lust, infatuation, friendship and gentle affection for the real thing. I truly believe that sex equals love, that the two of us are joined like the fishes in my glyph. I want to merge totally into my lover, for me there can be no barriers between us. Fluid and ever-changing, I become whatever my lover wants me to be. It's bliss when I'm so enmeshed I don't know where I end and my lover begins. My past partners all pull on my heart strings and I may have sex out of pity. With my watery sensitivity, I instinctively know what my partner is feeling and can respond to unspoken desires.

Pisces seeks: a soulmate, marriage, undying passion, romantic union.

Seduction technique: I mesmerise potential partners, drawing them in with my beddable eyes and promising them the world. A promise that could well be gone by morning.

Flirting: I flirt with everyone. It's my nature. A romantic at heart,

I enjoy the whole business of fishing for a partner. Although I flirt outrageously at every opportunity I could well be keeping my hand in or feel sorry for someone. No-one, even me, can tell the difference.

Trust and empathy: I naively trust everyone, even when it's patently obvious that I shouldn't, and I sympathise rather than empathise. I am promiscuously intimate.

Secret sexual desire: to be filmed dominating and possessing another soul.

Pisces as a partner

Partnership style: romantic and impractical, malleable and melding.

For me, the relationship is all. When it works it is blissful but I have an unhappy knack of becoming a victim to love. I don't tell my partner what I need, nor do I voice my disappointment when the relationship fails to live up to its romantic promise. Yearning for close relationship, I lose myself in my partner. In love with the idea of being in love, I tend to choose a partner because I am needed rather than because I am truly in love and I often find myself supporting my partner out of pity. Professing fidelity, in reality I have no problem carrying on two relationships at once. I desperately care about my partner, to such an extent that I may swallow them up, and I cannot conceive of being parted. The emotional ties bind me close. Or at least, they bind one part of me. There are two sides to my nature operating in tandem but going in opposite directions. The unconscious part does the opposite of the conscious. So, while I am swearing undying love, another part of me is casting around for a means of escape or another lover. I may even swim off altogether for a while, but I'll be back albeit to play the martyr. This is something that my partner quickly learns. It is never my fault, you can't blame me. I may leave emotionally but remain physically present, or I may leave physically and remain emotionally present. I find it impossible to cut the ties. I have no intention of hurting my partner, I just can't help myself.

What Pisces expects from partners: I see my partner as an extension of myself. Because I have emotionally merged, I expect my partner to instinctively know how I feel and what I need. I can't put my feelings into words, but I do want my partner to show a constant interest in how I am. I have a deep hunger for sympathy and compassion, and yearn for the consideration I show my partner to be reflected back to me. Sometimes I wish that my partner would fulfil my desire for utterly selfish sex as I usually spend all my time trying to make my partner happy, but I'm not going to say so.

When it ends: I don't actually end things. I stay in relationships long after it would have been sensible to leave! I may physically depart, sometimes for years, but the legal niceties are overlooked because somehow that would be too final, and anyway the emotional connection has never been broken. I still feel something for my partner, even if I'm living with someone else. Or I'm bound by guilt. The ties are never entirely cut. I may come swimming back, or not. It is all the same to elusive ol' me.

Pisces as a friend

Friendship style: emotional, intimate, intermittent.

I'm an exceptionally sympathetic friend, the perfect companion for a tear-jerker movie. I love the sentimental nostalgia of old black and white films. We can cry together, emote together, or wallow in self-pity if the mood takes us. I'll know exactly how you want your character to feel but may find it hard to separate reality from fantasy. I'm wonderfully understanding in a crisis but my tendency to wallow in it with your protagonist is not constructive. But if your character needs to make a confession, or seek absolution, see me. If your character has relationship troubles, there will be a sympathetic hearing but not necessarily sound advice. I'm excellent at telling your character how to conduct an affair behind a partner's back though. What I'll never willingly do is hurt your character, although my disappearing at crucial moments could well lead to a certain lack of trust between us. Months can elapse between our meetings, and when I return my full attention is focused on your character once more. I sashay from moment to moment and expect your character to be quietly waiting for my return. If not I'll act all martyred and hurt. Your character's reaction will of course be down to the sun-sign you've allocated.

Pisces as a co-worker

Co-worker Style: helpful, involved, emotional.

You need to grasp how much of a sacrifice I am prepared to make on your protagonist's behalf. I give my all, and then some. I don't have jealousy so I'll willingly help get a promotion and even take the blame for mistakes sometimes although I'll know it's not my fault. I offer compassion, understanding, sympathy, help, assistance, love and romance – all prettily packaged in a box marked 'guilt trip' if your character doesn't express undying appreciation afterwards. My nature compels me to make a burnt offering of myself. I so easily play the victim or the martyr. If I'm not called upon to save your character, I'll offer myself up regardless. But I have to warn you, your character relies on me at his or her peril. Just when needed most, I swim off. Check my promises have been kept!

By the light of the slipperiest moon

Pisces moon style: extremely sensitive, difficult to pin down.
Basic need: unity.

I'm such a sensitive little flower so please don't upset me. I swing between everyday consciousness and metaphysical awareness. My strongly developed intuition gives me enormous psychic gifts and considerable artistic abilities and I don't hesitate to use this to manipulate the world around me to suit my needs, but I find it hard to distinguish between true intuitions and my secret wishes. My emotions, especially guilt, are powerful currents that pull me this way and that without thought or reason. Lacking boundaries I am acutely aware of other people's pain, and am constantly invaded by their thoughts and feelings. I experience myself through emotional interaction with other people, and receive my emotional satisfaction through 'helping' others, although I admit I tend to keep them dependent on me. I often confuse pity with love, and sympathy with empathy. People tell me I'm too gullible for my own good. 'Real' life is a little too harsh for me so I seek solace in fantasy and what might have been – or in a bottle. I've got some deeply ingrained scripts around the victim-martyr-saviour-rescuer syndrome that need clearing and I often find myself caught up in addictions or compulsions. What nurtures me is feeding off other people although I yearn for total union with the divine.

Meeting the world

The Pisces mask: fluidity and graciousness.

When your character puts me on to face the world he or she may well be looking through a bottle, or gazing at a screen. I much prefer fantasy to reality and I escape whenever I can. I never know quite in which direction I'm moving and so easily make promises I can't keep just to make you feel happy at the time. Don't think you know me. I'm skilled at putting up a smokescreen. I'll be whatever you want, for a time. I seem to attract undesirable characters – bad boys or femme fatales are so much more seductive than goodie goodies – and they need me so. I'm prone to victim-martyr-saviour sub-plots, so much so that I can mask a tougher, more realistic sun-sign for awhile. An interesting conundrum arises when I have to take off my rose tinted glasses and extricate myself from my fantasies and face up to what is real in my world.

Pisces compatibility rating

Aries *; Taurus ****; Gemini ***; Cancer *****; Leo***; Virgo*****; Libra ****; Scorpio ****; Sagittarius*; Capricorn*; Aquarius*; Pisces *****

Further reading

Hall, Judy *The Astrology Bible,* Hamlyn

Hall, Judy *The Soulmate Myth: a dream come true or your worst nightmare* Flying Horse Publications

Hall, Judy *The Hades Moon: Pluto in aspect to the moon* Samuel Weiser

Hall, Judy *Patterns of the Past* and *Karmic Connections* Wessex Astrologer

Margesson, Maud *The Brontes and their Stars* (Rider, London, no date given) sadly this work is long out of print – my copy has a 1932 dedication – but second-hand copies may sometimes be obtained on the internet.

Data sources

Birth data used has been verified. Some birth data is unavailable. Only where a time is supported by direct evidence has a rising sign been given, rectified times have not been included. Sources are specified in the author's astrological texts or are to be found on Lois Rodden's astro-databank http://www.astro.com/astro-databank,

Acknowledgements

My deepest thanks to Margaret Cahill, Mario Reading, Christine Aziz and John Wadsworth for so freely sharing themselves through their blogs and for allowing extracts to be used in this book. My thanks also to all those who 'spoke their sign' or described a sign through their words and to those who gave permission for their words to be quoted. Every effort has been made to obtain permission for quotations from modern-day sources but it was not possible to contact some authors.

About the Author

An astrologer for 45 years, past-life and crystal specialist and holder of an M.A. in Cultural Astronomy and Astrology, Judy Hall has written 49 MBS books including the best selling *Crystal Bibles*, the *Astrology Bible* and one time-slip novel *Torn Clouds*. Another novel is in course of preparation. She has thrice appeared on the Watkins list of spiritually influential writers of the 21st century and is nominated for a Kindred Spirit 2013 lightworker award. She runs writing courses at her home in Dorset using her local landscape, her *Zodiac Pack* and astro-characterisation. www.judyhall.co.uk

**COMPASS
BOOKS**

Compass Books focuses on practical and informative 'how-to' books for writers. Written by experienced authors who also have extensive experience of tutoring at the most popular creative writing workshops, the books offer an insight into the more specialised niches of the publishing game.